The Go-Giver

Also by Bob Burg and John David Mann

Go-Givers Sell More

The Go-Giver Leader

Also by Bob Burg

Adversaries into Allies: Master the Art of Ultimate Influence

Endless Referrals: Network Your Everyday Contacts into Sales

The Success Formula

Also by John David Mann

Among Heroes (with Brandon Webb)

The Red Circle (with Brandon Webb)

The Slight Edge (with Jeff Olson)

Take the Lead (with Betsy Myers)

Flash Foresight (with Daniel Burrus)

The Secret Language of Money (with David Krueger, M.D.)

You Call the Shots (with Cameron Johnson)

The Go-Giver

*A Little Story About a
Powerful Business Idea*

Bob Burg and John David Mann

Expanded Edition

PORTFOLIO / PENGUIN

PORTFOLIO / PENGU I N
An imprint of Penguin Random House LLC
375 Hudson Street
New York, New York 10014
penguin.com

Foreword by Arianna Huffington published by arrangement with the author

Hardcover ISBN 978-1-59184-828-8
Special Markets ISBN 978-0-73521-800-0

Printed in the United States of America
10 9 8 7

Set in Apollo MT Std
Designed by Cassandra Garruzzo

To Mike and Myrna Burg
and Alfred and Carolyn Mann,
who gave us everything.

"Deeply heartfelt and meditative, *The Go-Giver* is filled with insights. More important, it accomplishes what few business books do—it reminds us of our own core humanity."

> —Ori Brafman, *New York Times* bestselling coauthor,
> *The Starfish and the Spider, Sway,* and *Click*

"At the heart of *The Go-Giver* is a philosophy—actually, a way of *being*—that will dramatically increase your business, enrich your life and make an extraordinary mark on the world around you."

> — Gary Keller, founder and chairman of the board, Keller Williams
> Realty, Intl; *New York Times* bestselling author, *The ONE Thing*

"Burg and Mann have crafted a business parable that is drawing comparisons with Dr. Spencer Johnson's wildly popular 1998 book, *Who Moved My Cheese?* . . . The world always needs a fresh approach to its most important messages. *The Go-Giver* is a great way to spread a positive and enriching message."

> —*Soundview Executive Book Alert*

"Most people don't have the guts to buy this book, never mind the will to follow through and actually use it. But you do. And I'm certain that you'll be glad you did."

> —Seth Godin, author of *Tribes* and *Linchpin*

"*The Go-Giver* has created such a buzz CEOs are buying it in bulk for their entire organizations. [The book] taps into a universal truth: Giving and receiving aren't mutually exclusive ideals."

> —*Huffington Post*

"*The Go-Giver* is the best business parable since *The Greatest Salesman in the World* and *The One Minute Manager*. This book shows that putting the other person first is the key to business success and personal fulfillment. It's also the most profitable."

> —Pat Williams, author, *Leadership Excellence;*
> senior vice president, the Orlando Magic

"*The Go-Giver* is filled with timeless truths practically presented that will positively transform every reader; it's a brilliant and easily read guide to doing good *and* doing well."

> —Rabbi Daniel Lapin, author, *Business Secrets from
> the Bible* and *Thou Shall Prosper*

"Trust is established when you act in the best interests of others. This terrific book wonderfully illuminates this and many other principles of contribution, abundance, service and success. In a style both engaging and insightful, *The Go-Giver* delivers a very powerful message."

—Stephen M. R. Covey, *New York Times*
bestselling author, *The Speed of Trust*

"Our deepest desire is to be taught and transformed by wisdom presented in its simplest form. Burg and Mann have mastered storytelling by returning us to the sacredness of our ancestors—giving, living and thriving while expressing passion for common sense."

— Temple Hayes, author, *When Did You Die?;*
spiritual leader and difference maker

"The greatest leader is a servant leader. *The Go-Giver* tells a great story about how to *serve* your way to success."

—John Addison, past co-CEO, Primerica, Inc.

"*The Go-Giver* is a lovely reminder to us all that the world is abundant and rewards those who act with a generosity of spirit."

—Lois P. Frankel, Ph.D., author, *See Jane Lead*
and *Nice Girls Don't Get the Corner Office*

"Similar to Mitch Albom's *Tuesdays with Morrie,* providing wisdom and insight on how to be more successful."

—*TheStreet.com*

"*The Go-Giver* does everything I would wish a good book to do. The story captured me from the very beginning to the very end. The lessons touched home again and again. Good books do that. This book does that. Read it to the very end."

—Michael E. Gerber, *New York Times* bestselling author, *The E-Myth*

"*The Go-Giver* should be handed out to every new college student as required reading."

—Angela Loehr Chrysler, CEO, Team National, Inc.;
director, National Companies, Inc.

"A classy and timeless read."

—Jones Loflin, coauthor, *Juggling Elephants*

"A quick read in the spirit of *The Greatest Salesman in the World* and *The One Minute Manager*. Burg and Mann write with a simple, informal style that offers a working-person's interpretation of the old adage 'give and you shall receive.'"

—*Publishers Weekly*

"*The Go-Giver* is a gem, filled with uncommon wisdom and five-star insights. A must-read book by anyone who wants to get more out of life."

—Gerhard Gschwandtner, founder and publisher, *Selling Power*

"*The Go-Giver* has had an enormous influence on how I do business and live my life, and I'm honored, humbled and grateful to share the Five Laws with others. Thank you for helping to make this world a better place, and me a better person!"

—Harriet E. Dominique, senior vice president, Corporate
Responsibility and Community Affairs, USAA

"Burg and Mann have demonstrated that adding value to people's lives is the way to climb the ladder of financial success. Focus on adding value to others and your own success will skyrocket."

—Fran Tarkenton, Hall of Fame quarterback;
founder and CEO, GoSmallBiz.com

"I don't know that I've ever read a more powerful book about succeeding in business and life."

—Gloria Loring, singer and actress; author,
Coincidence Is God's Way of Remaining Anonymous

"*The Go-Giver* hits a bull's-eye on the subject of success in business and life. Burg and Mann clearly understand how helping others succeed will help you succeed. I highly recommend this book."

—Dr. Ivan Misner, bestselling author, *Masters of Success;* founder, BNI

"For those who enjoy business parables, *The Go-Giver* is one of the more memorable books to come along."

—Editor's blog, *Soundview Executive Book Summaries*

"These five simple principles will help you achieve your goals and fulfill your dreams!"

—Brian Tracy, author, *The Psychology of Achievement*

"Short and sweet, this business parable packs a punch with its timely message of generosity. In our fast-paced world, we all need to be reminded of the genuine human spirit that builds the foundation for success. You'll love this book!"
—Nido Qubein, president, High Point University

"This book is exactly what is meant by the phrase 'Great things come in small packages.' The messages within these pages are treasures you will want to read over and over and share with all those you care about. These are the true keys to success in every aspect of life."
—Tom Hopkins, author, *How to Master the Art of Selling*

"A cross between *Jonathan Livingston Seagull* and *The 7 Habits of Highly Effective People* . . . an uplifting, quick read of a book that will appeal to customers who want to bring more heart and a holistic sense of mission to their livelihoods."
—*Retailing Insight*

"*The Go-Giver* taps into the secret that the mega-successful already know: Personal wealth is the by-product of making the world a better place."
—Paul Zane Pilzer, bestselling author, *The Wellness Revolution;* two-time U.S. presidential economic adviser

"This book makes a good first impression, and an even better second impression when you realize that the parable is deeper than you first thought."
—*Life Insurance Selling*

"Burg and Mann have taken the complicated game of business and infused it with clarity and purpose."
—Philip E. Harriman, CLU, ChFC, president, 2007 Million Dollar Round Table

"Deftly written and thoroughly reader-friendly . . . informed and informative as well as inspired and inspiring."
—*Midwest Book Review*

"The Five Laws are beautiful in their simplicity, but it is Mann and Burg's powerful storytelling that elevates them from the simply motivational to the truly inspirational."
—Scott Allen, columnist, *Fastcompany.com;* coauthor, *The Virtual Handshake*

CONTENTS

Foreword

Giving, touching others' lives, expanding the circle of our concern to include others, being authentic, and being always open to receiving as well as giving. That's not just a children's fairy tale—it's a good description of many of the most amazing people I've encountered.

And while they may live and work in different countries and in different fields, they all share the same core giving philosophy. This book captures that philosophy and shows that it is more than a fable, a parable, or a pipe dream. It's real—a path that people can follow in their daily lives.

People want to believe that this is the way the world *can* work: that living with a focus on others isn't just a nice goal but that it can be a way of life, and can lead to a life that is full, rich and fulfilling. But then, too often, we feel pressured by the voices (both external and internal) of cynicism and resignation, telling us, "It's a dog-eat-dog world out there—you've got to look out for #1."

Too many people think, "Oh, sure, once you've achieved success and financial stability, *then* you can afford to be a giving person!" But in this book, Bob Burg and John David

Mann—who, among other things, have given us the term *go-giver*—tell us that, in fact, being a giving person is how you achieve success in the first place, however you define success.

Too often people hear "be a giver" and think of charities and writing checks, of "giving back" once we have already done well for ourselves. But that's only one very specific facet of giving. By "be a giver," Bob and John mean be a giving person, *period:* one who gives thought, gives attention, gives care, gives focus, gives time and energy—gives *value* to others.

Not as a quid pro quo, not as a strategy to get ahead, but because it is, in and of itself, a satisfying and fulfilling way to be.

Arianna Huffington

Introduction to the Revised Edition

Not long after *The Go-Giver* first appeared, we got a letter from a man named Arlin Sorensen. The CEO of an Iowa IT firm, Arlin had organized a Go-Giver–themed summer retreat for more than two hundred peer-group companies. Inspired by the ideas in the book, several conference participants flew out to another state, on their own dime, to help brainstorm solutions for a colleague whose company was on the verge of closure. The firm pulled back from the brink and saw banner profits the following quarter—and the two men who'd done the consulting were surprised to find that what they learned in the process helped boost growth in their *own* companies, too.

All of which, Arlin told us, was a result of his reading our "little story about a powerful business idea."

And Arlin wasn't the only one sending us reports like this. People in all sorts of businesses started telling us that our story was changing the way they did things. Chambers of Commerce told us they were adopting Go-Giver precepts as part of their professional code and giving copies of the book to their members to help their businesses become more successful. A fitness club challenged its staff to continually come up with creative improvements in the business based on the book's core principles. A legal firm reported using the book to help more effectively negotiate matrimonial disputes.

The Go-Giver started as a book but soon became a movement. Our hero Joe's struggle to gain an advantage in his business (some "clout and leverage," as he put it) and his encounters with his mentor's counterintuitive principles describing how the world *really* works ("the more you give, the more you have") seemed to strike a chord—and not only in the world of business. Before long we were hearing from parents, teachers, pastors and counselors who were using the book in their work, and in their lives, too.

- A high school teacher in Indiana told us he was taking his school's senior class through the book because he found it "better equipped them to do well in the world." He has done it with every graduating class since.

- An executive chef at an exclusive Houston country club started using it to train his management team to reach even higher levels of excellence and member satisfaction.

- A Lithuanian expat in London moved back to her homeland and started her own publishing company just so she could share the book with her compatriots in their own language. "Your book will change our country," she told us.

From book clubs to executive councils, law firms to prayer groups, energy conglomerates to nursing homes, pizza shop managers to graduate school professors, people wrote to tell us how they were using the book. And it wasn't that they were saying they liked it. They were saying something better than that.

They were saying it *worked*.

Business owners told us the book helped them make their businesses more successful. In some cases, struggling businesses experienced a complete turnaround after implementing the "Five Laws of Stratospheric Success" Joe learns in these pages. Companies large and small started using it to train their sales and customer service teams to generate both more sales *and* happier customers. People reported using the Five Laws to great effect in their marriages and approach to parenting.

All of the foregoing might seem to suggest that the "secrets" in *The Go-Giver* must be startlingly new and original. They aren't, of course. The ideas here are as old as humanity. One of the messages we hear most often is some variation of "This is how I always *thought* (or always *hoped*) things worked. . . . I just never quite knew how to put it into words." When these readers crack open the pages of Joe's adventure, they tell us, they discover something they always knew somewhere inside themselves: that while the world may at times appear to be a dog-eat-dog place, there is actually a set of much kinder and vastly more powerful principles operating beneath the surface of casual appearances.

But don't take our word for it.

After reading what Joe and his mentor Pindar have to say, we invite you to take the next step and explore it for yourself.

Follow Pindar's Condition: test every law you read here and see what happens. "Not by thinking about it," as Pindar tells Joe in chapter 2, "not by talking about it, but by applying it in your life."

Enjoy—and our best wishes for your *stratospheric success*.

Bob Burg and John David Mann
October 2015

1: The Go-Getter

If there was anyone at the Clason-Hill Trust Corporation who was a go-getter, it was Joe. He worked hard, worked fast, and was headed for the top. At least, that was his plan. Joe was an ambitious young man, aiming for the stars.

Still, sometimes it felt as if the harder and faster he worked, the further away his goals appeared. For such a dedicated go-getter, it seemed like he was doing a lot of *going* but not a lot of *getting*.

Work being as busy as it was, though, Joe didn't have much time to think about that. Especially on a day like today—a Friday, with only a week left in the quarter and a critical deadline to meet. A deadline he couldn't afford *not* to meet.

Today, in the waning hours of the afternoon, Joe decided it was time to call in a favor, so he placed a phone call—but the conversation wasn't going well.

"Carl, tell me you're not telling me this . . ." Joe took a breath to keep the desperation out of his voice. "Neil Hansen?! Who the heck is Neil Hansen? . . . Well I don't care what he's offering, we can meet those specs . . . wait—c'mon, Carl, you owe me one! You know you do! Hey, who saved your bacon on the Hodges account? Carl, hang on . . . Carl!"

Joe clicked off the TALK button on his cordless phone and made himself calmly set down the instrument. He took a deep breath.

Joe was desperately trying to land a large account, an account he felt he richly deserved—one he *needed*, if he wanted to make his third-quarter quota. Joe had just missed his quota in the first quarter, and again in the second. Two strikes . . . Joe didn't even want to think about a third.

"Joe? You okay?" a voice asked. Joe looked up into the concerned face of his coworker Melanie Matthews. Melanie was a well-meaning, genuinely nice person. Which was exactly why Joe doubted she would survive long in a competitive environment like the seventh floor, where they both worked.

"Yeah," he said.

"Was that Carl Kellerman on the phone? About the BK account?"

Joe sighed. "Yeah."

He didn't need to explain. Everyone on the floor knew who Carl Kellerman was. He was a corporate broker looking for the right firm to handle an account Joe had nicknamed the Big Kahuna, or BK for short.

According to Carl, the boss at Big Kahuna didn't think Joe's firm had the "clout and leverage" to put the deal together. Now some character he'd never heard of had underbid and outperformed him. Carl claimed there was nothing he could do about it.

"I just don't get it," Joe said.

"I'm so sorry, Joe," said Melanie.

"Hey, sometimes you eat the bear . . ." He flashed a confident grin, but all he could think about was what Carl had said. As Melanie walked back to her desk, Joe sat lost in thought. *Clout and leverage . . .*

Moments later he leaped up and walked over to Melanie's desk. "Hey, Mel?"

She looked up.

"Do you remember talking with Gus the other day, something about a big wheel consultant giving a talk somewhere next month? You called him the Captain or something?"

Melanie smiled. "Pindar. The Chairman."

Joe snapped his fingers. "That's it! That's the guy. What's his last name?"

Melanie frowned. "I don't think . . ." She shrugged. "No, I don't think I've ever heard it mentioned. Everyone calls him the Chairman, or just Pindar. Why? You want to go hear the talk?"

"Yeah . . . maybe." But Joe was not interested in some lecture happening a month away. He was interested in only one thing—and that one thing needed to happen by the following Friday, when the third quarter came to an end.

"I was thinking, this guy is a real heavy hitter, right? Charges huge consulting fees, works only for the biggest and best firms? *Major* clout. I know we could handle the BK account, but I'm gonna need some big guns to win the deal back. I need *leverage.* Any idea how I can get a line to this Chairman guy's office?"

Melanie looked at Joe as if he were proposing to wrestle a grizzly bear. "You're just going to call him up?!"

Joe shrugged. "Sure. Why not?"

Melanie shook her head. "I have no idea how to contact him. Why don't you ask Gus?"

As Joe headed back to his desk, he wondered how Gus had managed to survive this long at Clason-Hill Trust. He never saw him do any actual *work*. Yet Gus had an enclosed office, while Joe, Melanie and a dozen others shared the open space of the seventh floor. Some said Gus had gotten his office because of seniority. Others said he'd earned it on merit.

According to office rumors, it had been years since Gus had sold a single account, and management kept him on purely out of loyalty. There were also whispers about Gus that went to the other extreme—that he had been supersuccessful in his younger days and was now an independently wealthy eccentric who stashed his millions away in mattresses while living a pensioner's lifestyle.

Joe didn't believe the rumors. He was pretty sure Gus brought in *some* accounts. But it was hard to picture him as a sales superstar. Gus dressed like a high school English teacher and reminded Joe more of a retired country doctor than of an active businessman. With his relaxed, easy manner, his long, rambling phone conversations with potential clients (conversations that seemed to touch on everything *but* business) and his erratic, extended vacations, Gus seemed like a relic of times long past.

Hardly a go-getter.

Joe stopped at Gus's open door and knocked softly.

"Come on in, Joe," came the reply.

"So you want to call right now and try to get in to see the man himself?" Gus thumbed carefully through his large Rolodex, found the dog-eared card he was searching for and copied the phone number onto a small slip of paper, which he then handed to Joe. He watched as Joe took the paper and punched in the number on his cordless phone.

"On a Friday afternoon?" Joe grinned. "Yup. I'm going to do exactly that."

Gus nodded thoughtfully. "One thing I have to say about you, Joe, you've got ambition, and I admire that." Gus absent-mindedly fingered a meerschaum pipe as he talked. "If there's anyone on this floor who's a go-getter, it's you."

Joe was touched. "Thanks, Gus." He headed back to his desk.

From behind him, Gus called out, "Don't thank me yet."

After a single ring, Joe was greeted by a cheerful voice belonging to a woman who identified herself as Brenda. He introduced himself, told her he needed to see the Chairman, and then readied himself to parry her stonewalling.

Instead, she shocked him by saying, "Of course he can meet with you. Can you come by tomorrow morning?"

"To—tomorrow?" he stammered. "On a Saturday?!"

"Yes, if that works with you. Is eight o'clock too early?"

Joe was stunned. "Don't . . . ah, don't you need to check with him first?"

"Oh, no," came her unruffled reply. "Tomorrow morning will be fine."

There was a brief silence. Joe wondered if she had him confused with someone else. Someone this Pindar character actually *knew*. "Ma'am?" he finally managed to say. "You, ah, you know this is my first time meeting with him, right?"

"Of course," she replied cheerfully. "You've heard about his Trade Secret, and you want to learn about it."

"Well, yes, that's it, more or less," he replied. Trade Secret? The man was willing to share his Trade Secret? He could hardly believe his good fortune.

"He'll meet with you one time," continued Brenda. "After that, if you agree to his conditions, he'll want to set up additional appointments to actually show you the Secret."

"Conditions?" Joe was crestfallen. He was sure these "conditions" would involve a stiff consulting fee or retainer he couldn't afford. And even if he could, it might require the kind of high-level credentials Joe certainly didn't have. Was it even worth it to go on? Or should he cut his losses and find a graceful way to back out now?

"Of course," he replied. "Oh, and what are his, ah, conditions, again?"

"You'll have to hear that directly from the Old Man," she said with a giggle.

Joe took down the address she gave him, mumbled his thanks and clicked off the phone. In less than twenty-four hours he was going to meet with—what had she called him?— the Old Man.

And why had she giggled when she said that?

2: The Secret

The next morning Joe arrived at the address Brenda had given him and pulled up into the huge circular drive. He couldn't help being impressed as he parked and looked up at the beautiful stone mansion that stretched up a good four stories in front of him. He gave a low whistle. This was some place. The man had *clout*, all right.

Joe had done his homework the night before. An hour on the Internet had told him some pretty remarkable things about the person he was about to meet.

The man known as the Chairman had had a very successful career with a wide range of enterprises. Now mostly retired from his own companies, he devoted most of his time to teaching and mentoring others. He was in great demand as a consultant to Fortune 500 CEOs and as a keynote speaker at top-shelf corporate events. He had become something of a legend. One article had dubbed him "the business world's best-kept secret."

"Talk about clout," thought Joe. "Leverage, big time!"

"Joe! Welcome!"

A slender man with neatly combed graying-black hair, a

pale blue shirt, light gray jacket and pressed, light gray slacks stood outside the great oak door. Early sixties, Joe guessed, maybe even late fifties. The man's age was one detail the Internet search had not yielded.

His precise net worth was another, but by all accounts, it was *stratospheric*. The castle that stood before Joe confirmed that impression, as did the man's stately, elegant presence. From his beaming expression, it was clear that his "Welcome!" was genuine and not just a figure of speech.

"Good morning, sir," said Joe. "Thank you for taking the time to see me."

"You're welcome—and thank *you*, for exactly the same reason." Pindar smiled broadly over his firm handshake. Joe returned a somewhat bewildered smile of his own and wondered, "Why is *he* thanking *me*?"

"Let's head over to the terrace for a hot cup of Rachel's famous coffee," said Joe's host as he ushered him onto a small slate path that led around the side of the mansion. "Surprised to be here?"

"Actually, yes," Joe admitted. "I'm just wondering how many business legends would open their homes to a perfect stranger on a Saturday morning."

Pindar nodded as they walked along the path. "Actually, successful people do this all the time. Typically, the more successful they are, the more willing they are to share their secrets with others."

Joe nodded, trying his best to believe that this could possibly be true.

Pindar glanced at him, then smiled again. "Appearances can be deceiving, Joe. In fact, they nearly always are."

They walked for a moment before Pindar continued. "I was sharing a stage once with Larry King—you know, the radio and television interviewer?"

Joe nodded.

"And since he'd interviewed so many famous, successful and powerful people, I thought I'd check my own observations against his. 'Larry,' I asked, 'are your guests as genuinely nice as they seem? Even the real superstars?' He fixed me with a gaze and said, 'Tell you what. The interesting thing is, the bigger they are, the nicer they are.'"

Something about Pindar's warm, raspy voice had put Joe curiously at ease from the first moment he heard it. Now he identified that something: it was a *storyteller's voice*.

Pindar continued. "Well, Larry thought for a moment about what he'd said, and then he said more. 'I believe that a person can reach a certain level of success without being particularly special. But to get really, really big, to reach the kind of *stratospheric success* we're talking about, people need to have something on the inside, something that's genuine.'"

As they arrived at the terrace table, Joe glanced around—and just managed not to gasp out loud. Beyond the city stretching below them to the west lay a range of long, rolling mountains, half-shrouded in cottony clouds. The view took Joe's breath away.

They took their seats, and the young woman Pindar had called Rachel appeared with a pot of her "famous" coffee. As she poured cups for both of them, Joe thought, "Susan won't believe it when I tell her about this place." He had told his wife only that he was going to "meet with a potential client." He smiled as he pictured the expression that would light up her face when she heard about his adventure.

"Wow," said Joe. "Larry King, huh? By the way, this coffee is spectacular. Is Rachel's coffee really famous?"

"It is in this home," Pindar said with a smile. "I'm not a betting man, but if I were, you know what I'd bet?"

Joe shook his head.

"I'd bet that one day it will be famous worldwide. Rachel is very special. Been with us for about a year now, but I expect she'll be leaving us before long. I've been encouraging her to open a chain of coffeehouses. Her coffee is too good not to share with the world."

"I can see what you mean." Joe leaned in and adopted his best confidential, just-us-guys-talking manner. "If she could reproduce this on an industrial scale, you two could make a killing." He sat back in his chair and took another sip.

Pindar set his cup down and looked at Joe thoughtfully.

"Actually, Joe, in the brief time we have this morning, that's where I want to begin. You and I are coming from two different directions when it comes to wealth creation. If we're going to take this walk together, we need to start by facing the same direction. If you notice, what I said was 'share her coffee.' What you said was 'make a killing.' Do you see the difference?"

Joe wasn't sure if he did or not, but he cleared his throat and said, "Yes . . . I think so."

Pindar smiled. "Please don't misunderstand me. There's

nothing wrong with making money. Lots of it, in fact. It's just not a goal that will make you successful." Reading the bewilderment on Joe's face, he nodded and put his hand up to signal that he would explain. "You want to understand success, yes?"

Joe nodded.

"All right. I'm going to share my Trade Secret with you now." Pindar leaned forward a bit and softly spoke one word.

"Giving."

Joe waited for more, but apparently, that was it. "I beg your pardon?"

Pindar smiled.

"Giving?" repeated Joe.

Pindar nodded.

"That's the secret to your success? Your Trade Secret? *Giving?*"

"Indeed," said Pindar.

"Ah," said Joe. "Well, that's . . . that's . . ."

"'That's too simple, even if it were true, which it can't possibly be'?" asked Pindar. "Is that what you're thinking?"

"Something like that," Joe admitted sheepishly.

Pindar nodded. "Most people have that reaction. In fact, most people just laugh when they hear that the secret to success is *giving*." He paused. "Then again, most people are nowhere near as successful as they wish they were."

Joe certainly couldn't argue that point.

"You see," Pindar continued, "the majority of people operate with a mindset that says to the fireplace, 'First give me some heat, *then* I'll throw on some logs.' Or that says to the bank, 'Give me interest on my money, *then* I'll make a deposit.' And of course, it just doesn't work that way."

Joe frowned, trying to parse the logic of Pindar's examples.

"You see? You can't go in two directions at once. Trying to be successful with making money as your goal is like trying to travel a superhighway at seventy miles an hour with your eyes glued to the rearview mirror." He took another thoughtful sip and waited for Joe to process this thought.

Joe felt as if his brain were going seventy on the highway—in reverse. "Okay," he began slowly, "so you're saying, successful people keep their focus on what they're . . . giving, sharing, whatever," he saw Pindar nod, "and *that's* what creates their success?"

"Exactly," cried Pindar. "*Now* we're facing the same direction!"

"But . . . wouldn't an awful lot of people take advantage of you?"

"Excellent question." Pindar set his cup down and leaned forward. "Most of us have grown up seeing the world as a place of limitation rather than as a place of inexhaustible treasures. A world of competition rather than one of co-creation." He saw that Joe was puzzled again. "Dog eat dog," he explained. "As in, 'Oh, sure, we all act polite on the surface, but let's face it, it's really every man for himself.' That about sum it up?"

Joe admitted that it did about sum it up indeed. That's certainly what he believed, anyway.

"Well," said Pindar, "it's simply not true." He noted Joe's

skeptical look and continued. "Have you ever heard people say, *You can't always get what you want*?"

Joe grinned. "You mean, the Rolling Stones?"

Pindar smiled. "Actually, I imagine people were saying that well before Mick Jagger's time. But yes, that's the general idea."

"You're not going to tell me *that's* not true, are you? That we actually *do* get what we want?"

"No," said Pindar, "that one *is* true. In life, you often *don't* get what you want. But," he leaned forward again and his voice grew softer with emphasis, "here's what you *do* get— *You get what you expect*."

Joe frowned again, trying to mentally test out the truth of this last thought.

Pindar leaned back and sipped his coffee, watching Joe. After a moment's silence, he continued.

"Or put it another way: *What you focus on is what you get*. You've heard the expression 'Go looking for trouble and that's what you'll find'?"

Joe nodded.

"It's true, and not only about trouble. It's true about *everything*. Go looking for conflict, and you'll find it. Go looking for people to take advantage of you, and they generally will. See the world as a dog-eat-dog place, and you'll always find a bigger dog looking at you as if you're his next meal. Go looking for the best in people, and you'll be amazed at how much talent, ingenuity, empathy and goodwill you'll find.

"Ultimately, the world treats you more or less the way you expect to be treated."

Pindar paused for a moment to let Joe absorb that thought, then added one more.

"In fact, Joe, you'd be amazed at just how much *you* have to do with what happens *to* you."

Joe drew a breath. "So," he spoke this next thought slowly, thinking it through out loud, "you're saying, people don't take advantage of you because you don't expect them to? That because you don't put any focus on selfishness and greed, even when it's all around you, it doesn't have much impact on you?" Then he had a flash of inspiration. "Like a healthy immune system—the disease is all around you, but you don't catch it?"

Pindar's eyes sparkled. "Wonderful! That's an exquisite way of putting it." He kept talking as he scribbled in a little notebook he had produced from inside his jacket. "I have to remember that. You mind if I use that bit of brilliance?"

"No, go ahead," Joe gestured grandly, "take my brilliance. I'm full of it." He paused, then added, "Least that's what my wife always says."

Pindar burst out laughing as he slipped his little notebook back into the unseen pocket. He put both hands on his knees and looked directly at the younger man.

"Joe, I'd like to do something with you. I'd like to show you what I call my Five Laws of Stratospheric Success. If you can make a little time, say, every day for a week."

"Seriously?" Joe nearly stuttered. "For a week? I . . . I don't know how much time I can take off. . . ."

Pindar waved his hand vaguely, as if to say, *Time means*

14

nothing. "Not a problem. All we'll need is one hour a day. Your lunch hour. You do take time for lunch every day?"

Joe nodded, dumbfounded. The man was going to meet with him every day for a week? And hand over the details of his most valuable Trade Secret?!

"First, though," Pindar continued, "first you'll need to agree to my conditions."

Joe's heart sank. The conditions. He had forgotten all about that. It was only after he agreed to Pindar's conditions, Brenda had said, that they would set up further meetings.

Joe gulped. "I really don't have the means—"

Pindar held up his hands. "Please, don't worry, it's nothing like that."

"So," Joe began, "do I need to sign an NDA or . . . ?"

This brought a big, booming laugh from Pindar. "No, no non-disclosure agreements—if anything, the opposite. I call these Five Laws my Trade Secret, not because I don't want people to find them, but for exactly the opposite reason. I call them my Trade Secret so that people *will* find them—so they'll *seek* them. So they'll place the proper value on them. Because it's really a term of honor."

"Excuse me?" Joe was lost.

Pindar smiled. "The word itself. *Secret.* Originally, it meant something treasured—something sifted, weighed and *set apart* for its special value. Actually, if I had my way, *everyone* would know these Five Laws.

"In fact," he added, "that's exactly why I have put these

conditions in place. Actually, it's just one Condition. Are you ready?"

Joe nodded.

"I need you to agree that you will test every Law I show you by *actually trying it out*. Not by thinking about it, not by talking about it, but by applying it in your life."

Joe started to give his assent, but Pindar stopped him and continued.

"And that's not all. You must apply each Law *right away, the same day you first learn it*."

Joe looked at Pindar to see if he was kidding. "Seriously? Before I go to sleep that night? Or I'll turn into a pumpkin?"

Pindar's face relaxed into a grin. "No, you have a point, you won't turn into a pumpkin. But if you don't abide by my Condition, our meetings will come to an end."

"But," Joe stammered, "not to sound impertinent, how would you know?"

"Another excellent question. How would I know?" Pindar nodded thoughtfully. "I wouldn't. But you would. It's the honor system. If you don't find a way to apply each Law I show you the very same day you learn it, I'll trust that the next morning, you'll call Brenda to cancel the rest of our appointments."

He looked at Joe.

"I have to know you're taking this seriously. But here's what's far more important: *you* have to know you're taking this seriously."

Joe nodded slowly. "I think I understand. You want to make sure I'm not wasting your time. Fair enough."

Pindar smiled. "Joe, no offense, but you don't have that power."

Joe looked confused.

"I mean, the power to waste my time. Only *I* can do that. And truthfully, it's a vice I gave up a long time ago. The reason for my Condition is that I don't want to see you wasting *your* time."

Joe looked down and saw Pindar's outstretched hand. He took it and gave it a firm shake. He felt a thrill go through him, as if he had just embarked on an adventure worthy of Indiana Jones, and mirrored the Chairman's broad smile with one of his own.

"You've got a deal."

3: The Law of Value

Just before noon that Monday, Joe arrived at the great stone mansion eager to see what lay in store. All he knew was that he would be meeting with Pindar and a friend of his, a real estate magnate who had agreed to talk with Joe about the First Law of Stratospheric Success.

Joe still wondered about this whole "giving" business and whether or not this Trade Secret contained anything that would really work for him.

"But it's sure working for Pindar," he mused as he drove up the broad, tree-lined drive. And it wasn't just the man's résumé and magnificent property. "The guy *radiates* success," he thought. "It's not just money, it's something far more powerful than money."

He had thought about nothing else all weekend and still couldn't quite identify what that "something" was.

Pindar stood waiting for him as he rounded the circular drive and pulled up to the stone steps. Before Joe could cut the engine, Pindar opened the passenger's door and hopped in.

"Okay if we take your car? Don't want to be late for our meeting."

Joe felt a stab of disappointment. He wasn't going to get any of Rachel's famous coffee after all.

"Here," said Pindar as he buckled himself into his seat and handed over a giant mug of steaming hot coffee. "You can enjoy this along the way."

Twenty minutes later they arrived downtown and parked at Iafrate's Italian-American Café. Obviously much more than a café, the full-service restaurant was jammed, with a line forming at the door.

On their way into the building, someone pushed gruffly past them, complaining about how crowded it was, and bumped into Pindar. Much to Joe's surprise, Pindar simply smiled at him.

The moment they were inside the door, the maître d' came over and escorted the two of them to a corner table.

"Of course," thought Joe, "Pindar must be a VIP here."

"Thank you, Sal," said Pindar. Sal bowed to Pindar and winked at Joe. It struck Joe that Pindar was exceedingly gracious to everyone they encountered, and, as they took their seats, Joe asked Pindar about that.

"It never hurts to be kind to people," Pindar replied. "Once when I was a young man, I was walking to a young lady's home to meet her for our very first date. I was nervous. As I turned onto her street, an older man walked right into me, banging his head into mine and tromping on my foot. He was embarrassed that he hadn't been watching where he was going and mortified that he might have injured me. 'No harm done,' I assured him. 'I've been told I have a hard head—I hope you didn't hurt yourself!' He laughed with surprise. I wished him a wonderful day and hurried on to meet my young lady friend.

"About fifteen minutes after I'd arrived at the girl's home, I heard the front door open. 'Daddy!' she called out, 'I want you to meet my date.'"

Pindar stopped and glanced at Joe as if expecting him to finish the story.

Joe did. "And let me guess—it was the man who had smacked into you?"

"It was," agreed Pindar, "back from a quick trip to the store. He complimented his daughter on her good judgment and told her I was a thoughtful, polite young man."

"So, you could say your relationship got off on the right foot," observed Joe.

Pindar laughed. "Indeed it did. Stayed that way, too. That beautiful young lady has been my wife for nearly fifty years. . . . Ernesto!"—he called out to one of the cooks who was headed their way. *"Buon giorno, caro,"* Pindar exclaimed.

The portly fellow beamed and hunkered down with them at their table.

"You gonna introduce me to your new friend?" Ernesto's voice bore traces of a crisp Northern Italian accent.

"Ernesto, this is Joe. Joe, Ernesto."

A young waiter approached with a pair of menus, but before Joe or Pindar could say a word, Ernesto turned to the young man and fired off a soft stream of Italian phrases. The waiter whooshed silently away again.

"Ernesto," said Pindar, "tell my young friend how you got started here."

Ernesto looked at Joe and said, "Hot dogs."

Joe blinked. "Hot dogs?"

"I came here," Ernesto went on, "ah, must be more than twenty years ago now, a foolish young man. I had just enough money saved to buy a hot dog cart and the license to run it. Actually, come to think of it, the license cost me more than the cart!"

Pindar chuckled, and Joe had the distinct sense that his host had heard this story many times before.

"It was hard, at first," Ernesto was saying, "but I had some loyal customers, and word got around. After a few years, my little cart got written up in the city's annual *Best of* guide."

The chef paused to glance back toward the grill.

"Wow. Really?" said Joe. "Best hot dog stand in the city? That's great."

Pindar smiled and gently corrected him: "Best outdoor dining *experience* in the city."

Ernesto held up both hands modestly and shrugged. "They were kind to me."

"But," Joe stammered, "how did you do that? I mean, no offense, but how does a hot dog stand manage to outrank the swanky sidewalk cafés in this neighborhood?"

Ernesto gave another theatrical shrug, his eyebrows and shoulders moving together like a marionette saying, *Who knows?* He winked at Pindar. "Lucky?" He glanced back at the grill again. *"Scusi uno momento—"* and he stood up and strode away.

"Quite a character," Joe noted aloud as they watched Ernesto disappear through a door to the kitchen.

Pindar nodded. "Indeed he is. Actually, Ernesto is the head chef here."

"Really," said Joe.

"Really," Pindar replied. "In fact, he owns the place."

"Really." Joe was intrigued.

Their waiter placed their food before them and Pindar thanked him. He took his first bite of eggplant parmigiana, closed his eyes and groaned with pleasure. "The man is an artist."

"It's delicious," Joe agreed. As he dove into the magnificent meal, he thought of how Susan would love this place. The two men ate in silence for nearly a minute before Pindar spoke again.

"In fact, he owns a half dozen restaurants now. Also several hundred million dollars' worth of commercial real estate. All starting with a hot dog stand."

Joe dropped his silverware and stared at Pindar, who continued savoring his lunch. *"He's* the guy we came here to meet? The real estate magnate is *him*?!"

Ernesto was headed back toward their table as Pindar whispered to Joe, "A very useful thing to remember: *appearances can be deceiving.*" He slid over to make room for the chef. *"Truth is, they nearly always are."*

Ernesto slipped into the booth next to Pindar. Over the

next five minutes, he and Pindar gave Joe a quick history of his career.

Young Ernesto Iafrate's reputation had grown until he was "discovered" by several business executives, who abandoned the local high-class establishments to have their power lunches at the little sidewalk hot dog stand.

Although Ernesto rarely talked about himself, one of these regulars—a man whom Ernesto called simply "the Connector" (Joe made a mental note to ask Pindar later about this mysterious-sounding character)—eventually learned of his background as a chef. Impressed with the young man's sharp business mind and exceptional devotion to service, a few of these executives pulled together an investment group and backed him with the finances to open his own restaurant.

"And within a few years," Pindar interjected, "his little café did so well that he bought us out, earning us all a tidy profit in the process."

And he hadn't stopped there. After establishing a group of area restaurants, Ernesto began investing some of his profits in the properties adjoining his restaurants. Over the years, he became one of the largest commercial real estate owners in the city.

As he listened, Joe realized there was another layer to Ernesto that he hadn't seen at first. Underneath that jovial, bigger-than-life Italian chef persona there was a powerful sense of focus and intention. Once Joe became aware of it, it was riveting. He began to see why the little group of executives had invested in the man's future.

Joe understood that Pindar had emphasized the word "experience" for a reason. It was not the hot dogs but the person serving the hot dogs that had vaulted the young man to such popularity. Not the dining—the dining *experience.* Ernesto had made buying a hot dog into an unforgettable event.

Especially for children, Pindar pointed out.

"I've always been good at remembering kids' names," Ernesto explained.

"And remembering their birthdays," continued Pindar. "And their favorite colors, and their favorite cartoon heroes, and their best friends' names." He glanced at Joe and gave the next word emphasis: "Et cetera."

Ernesto gave another trademark shrug. "What can I say? I like kids."

Children started dragging their parents to the little hot dog stand. Soon the parents were dragging their friends there, too. It turned out that Ernesto was just as gifted at remembering adults' interests as he was with kids.

"Everyone likes to be appreciated," said Ernesto.

"And that's the Golden Rule of business," added Pindar. *"All things being equal—"*

Ernesto finished the phrase: "*—people will do business with and refer business to those people they know, like and trust.*"

He turned to look at Joe. "Tell me, what distinguishes a good restaurant from a great restaurant? Why do some restaurants do well, while a few, like this one, do *stratospherically* well?"

"Obviously, better food," replied Joe without hesitation.

Ernesto's delighted laughter filled the booth. Several heads turned and a wave of smiles rolled through the dining room like ripples on a pond.

"Ahh, *mille grazie, signore,* you are a man of good taste! But I have to admit, while our food is very good, there are half a dozen other places within three blocks with food just as wonderful as ours. Still, even on their best nights, they're lucky to have half the clientele that comes here. Why is that, do you think?"

Joe had no answer.

"A bad restaurant," Ernesto went on, "tries to give *just enough* food and service, both in quantity and quality, to justify the money it takes from the customer. A good restaurant strives to give the *most* quantity and quality for the money it takes.

"But a *great* restaurant—ahh, a *great* restaurant strives to defy imagination! Its goal is to provide *a higher quality of food and service than any amount of money could possibly pay for.*" He looked at Pindar, then back at Joe. "Did the Old Man tell you he would show you his Five Laws?"

Joe nodded eagerly. He was about to learn the First Law of Stratospheric Success!

Ernesto looked again at Pindar. "Should I tell him?"

"Please," replied Pindar.

Ernesto leaned in and spoke in a conspiratorial whisper:

> *"Your true worth is determined by*
> *how much more you give in value*
> *than you take in payment."*

Joe wasn't sure how to respond. Giving away more value than you get paid for? *That* was their big secret?

"I'm sorry . . . I don't get it," Joe confessed. "I mean, I appreciate where you're coming from, and your story is obviously . . . well, it's amazing. But honestly, that sounds like a recipe for bankruptcy! It's almost like you're trying to *avoid* making money."

"Not at all." Ernesto waggled one finger. "'Does it make money?' is not a bad question. It's a *great* question. It's just a bad *first* question. It starts you off pointed in the wrong direction."

He let Joe ponder that for a moment, then continued.

"The *first* question should be, 'Does it serve? Does it add value to others?' If the answer to that question is yes, *then* you can go ahead and ask, 'Does it make money?'"

"In other words," said Joe, "exceed people's expectations, and they'll pay you even more."

"That's one way to look at it," replied Ernesto, "but the point isn't to have them pay you more, it's to *give* them more. You give, give, give. Why?" Another shrug. "Because you love to. It's not a strategy, it's a way of life. And when you do," he added with a big grin, "then very, very profitable things begin to happen."

"Wait," said Joe. "So, 'profitable things begin to happen' —but I thought you said you're not thinking about the results."

"That's right," Ernesto agreed, "you're not. But that doesn't mean they won't happen!"

"And they certainly will," added Pindar. "All the great fortunes in the world have been created by men and women who had a greater passion for what they were *giving*—their product, service or idea—than for what they were *getting*. And many of those great fortunes have been squandered by others who had a greater passion for what they were *getting* than what they were *giving*."

Joe grappled with everything he'd heard. It seemed to make sense—at least, when these two characters were saying it. But as far as he could see, it just didn't square with his experience. "I have a hard time seeing how—"

"Ah," said Pindar, holding up his index finger and cutting Joe off mid-sentence.

Joe blanched. "What?"

Ernesto grinned. He leaned in toward Joe and said, "Did he tell you about his, you know—*Condition*?"

Joe looked puzzled for a moment, and then he understood. "Oh, right. The Condition."

Pindar smiled. "It's not about *seeing*. It's about *doing*."

Joe sighed. "Right," he repeated. "I need to find some way to apply it." He looked at both men, then added, "or I'll turn into a pumpkin."

The two men chuffed with glee, and Joe felt his face relax into a grin, too. For the moment, he had forgotten all about his secret quest for *clout and leverage*.

Pindar was already on his feet. "We should go. This young man needs to get back to work."

"Who are you seeing tomorrow?" Ernesto asked Joe.

Joe looked at Pindar.

"Tomorrow, a bona fide genius," replied Pindar. "The CEO."

"Ahhh," said Ernesto, nodding, "the CEO. Very good. *Very* good. Keep your ears open, young man."

The CEO! Joe tried to imagine who this person might be.

THE LAW OF VALUE

Your true worth is determined by how much more you give in value than you take in payment.

4: The Condition

On his solitary drive back to the office after returning Pindar to his home, Joe felt his head swirl. He kept replaying snippets of his lunch, reexamining Ernesto's story and trying to penetrate the mystery that lay at the heart of it. He knew the key was in there. Somehow, he just couldn't see it.

So far these Five Laws of Stratospheric Success sounded like something Joe might more likely have picked up from Mr. Rogers than from Warren Buffett.

You give, give, give. Why? Because you love to. It's not a strategy, it's a way of life.

As he pondered these thoughts, Joe felt a persistent tug in the back of his mind. It wasn't until he was seated at his desk, going through his usual routines, that he realized what that nagging thought was.

Clout and leverage.

His third-quarter quota! He needed to come up with a way to land the BK account before Friday. Were his meetings with Pindar getting him any closer to that goal? He thought back to his first meeting with Pindar on Saturday—

And groaned.

The *Condition*.

Joe looked around at his coworkers, as if worried that someone might have noticed his groan or even heard his thoughts.
The Condition. He was supposed to apply the Law of Value
right away, before the day was out.

But how?

His cordless phone rang and he snapped it off the desk.
"Joe here."

"Joe, hey, it's Jim Galloway."

Joe's heart sank when he heard the apologetic tone in Jim's
voice. Galloway was a lawyer Joe worked with now and then.
They had played tennis a few times, doubles with Susan and
Jim's wife. Jim was a good guy. And from the tone of his
voice, Joe guessed he was calling to break the news that Joe's
company was not getting the contract renewal for a multina-
tional firm Jim represented.

"I'm sorry, buddy, I tried. They say they need someone
with stronger overseas connections. I just hung up with them.
Wasn't much I could do."

First the BK account, and now this! Joe was careful not to
let his disappointment seep into his voice. "No problem, Jim.
Next time." He started to hang up, then brought the phone
back to his ear and said, "Hey, Jim?" He waited a moment,
then heard the voice on the other end.

"Joe?"

"Yeah, Jim—hang on a sec." He reached down and opened
his bottom drawer, where he kept a strategic business card

file on the competition. These cards represented the people it was his daily mission to beat to the punch. After a short search, he found the one he was looking for.

He stared at the card and thought, "Give more in value, huh? Well, here goes nothing."

"Jim? Here, try this guy. Ed Barnes, B-A-R-N-E-S. I heard he's pretty strong overseas. . . . Yes, he's a competitor. I just thought he might be in a better position to help." Joe didn't know if he felt more like laughing or crying at the words coming out of his mouth. "No, you don't owe me, Jim. I just hope it works out. Sorry we couldn't help this time."

He clicked off the phone, set it on his desk and stared at it, lost in disbelief at what he'd just done.

"This guy just blows me off—and I give him a *referral*?" he muttered. "And throw some good business at a *competitor*?!"

He glanced up and saw Gus at his office door, gazing at him. Gus smiled and nodded.

Joe nodded back and got busy with paperwork.

5: The Law of Compensation

When Joe appeared the next day at noon at the reception desk for Learning Systems for Children, Inc., he was met by a robust woman in her late sixties with a huge brass nameplate on her desk that read simply MARGE.

"Here ta meet the CEO, are ya?" she chirped, and without waiting for an answer, stuck out her hand. "Marge."

"Yes," admitted Joe, shaking the proffered hand. He looked around nervously, wondering where Pindar was. "Am I early?"

"Yer friend, Mr. Pindar? He left a message, said he'll be right along. Dontcha worry. I'll setcha right up in th' conference room. Nicole'll be in ta see after you, bring you a cuppa joe . . ." She laughed at her own inadvertent joke—"Joe!"

Joe followed the woman down a bright corridor. She opened the door to the conference room; Joe began to step inside— and stopped dead in his tracks. What on earth?

This was like no conference room Joe had ever seen.

He had expected to find a long mahogany conference table, polished to a sheen, equipped with the latest in teleconferencing units. Instead, the room was lined with small wooden tables littered with tubs of modeling clay, pipe cleaners of all colors, piles of construction paper and an endless array of crayons. A row of kids' easels ran along the walls, plastered with finger paintings. More finger paintings decorated the walls.

But it wasn't the way the room was furnished that left Joe staring.

It was the chaos that filled the room.

About a dozen people, ranging in age from their late twenties to early sixties, stood talking and laughing at once, all of them busily engaged in what looked to Joe like the delirious pursuit of making a mess. Some smooshed together lumps of modeling clay, others smeared finger paints on the easels. One woman gazed at the inscrutable tangle of pipe cleaners she held in one hand, as serious as Hamlet regarding Yorick's skull.

Joe gaped. He had stepped out of the world of corporate culture and fallen back through time to a kindergarten classroom.

"Whoops." Without batting an eye, Marge simply closed the door again and marched down the hall to the next room, beckoning Joe to follow. "Other conference room, I guess."

In a daze, Joe managed to mumble his thanks as Marge clicked the door closed behind him.

Joe found himself alone in a room outfitted much like the one he'd just seen. He walked slowly to the center of the room, marveling at the sheer exuberance and unbridled energy of the artwork that covered the walls.

The door softly clicked open. Joe whirled to find himself face-to-face with a smiling young woman. Joe caught a smoky, familiar scent, and saw that she carried a glass press-pot of coffee.

"Hi, I'm Nicole." She flashed a smile that made Joe want to reach for his sunglasses. "You must be Joe?"

Joe nodded.

"Pindar called; he'll be here in two minutes. Would you like some coffee while you wait? It's likely to be the best coffee you've ever tasted."

"Please." Joe finally found his voice again. "Thank you." As Nicole began pouring a cup for him, he looked around the room and asked, "So am I really going to meet with the CEO?"

"That's what I hear," she replied.

"Yes, but I mean, are we really meeting *in here*?"

She glanced around. "It is a little different, isn't it?"

"A little," said Joe. "It's . . . wild."

"Thanks," she said.

Joe looked at her in surprise. "You had something to do with this?"

She looked all around the room, appreciatively noting every detail. "I came up with the design of the room and pretty much put it all together."

"Let me guess—you have kids?"

She let loose with a laugh like honey. "Do I ever! Seems like millions." She noticed Joe's expression and laughed again. "Grade school. I'm a teacher," she explained. "Used to be, anyway, before I worked here."

Joe glanced at the walls again.

Nicole smiled. "Believe it or not, adults really do meet in this room, and they get quite a lot done. You wouldn't believe what finger painting and modeling clay can do for a bunch of stuck-in-their-heads grownups."

"I guess," Joe said. He nodded toward the room next door. "So was that a . . . ?" Joe struggled to find a way to finish his question. Was that a *what*? "A focus group or something? Parents?"

Nicole smiled. "Those are the company's top marketing executives. They're brainstorming ideas for opening the next group of overseas markets."

The company's top marketing executives?! Before Joe could ask more, he heard the quiet whoosh of the opening door and the warm rasp of that familiar storyteller's voice.

"Hello?" Pindar stepped into the room, strode over to the young woman and warmly took her hand in his. "Nicole! Thanks so much for making the time to meet my young friend. I told him he needed to talk with a bona fide genius!"

The woman blushed.

A bona fide genius? Joe tried his best to hide his astonishment. He'd *already been talking* with the CEO.

"Nicole," Pindar continued, "please meet Joe, my newest friend. Joe, Nicole Martin. Nicole runs one of the most successful educational software companies in the country."

"But—but you're so young!" Joe felt a little foolish saying this, but the woman looked about his own age.

"Not nearly as young as my customers," she replied with a smile.

Pindar sat down cross-legged at one of the low wooden

tables and began rummaging around in the large paper sack he'd carried in with him.

"We market a series of learning programs to school systems throughout the United States, Canada and thirteen other countries," Nicole explained. "But don't worry," she added, flashing that dazzling smile, "one of these days, we're really going to be big."

While Nicole spoke, Pindar drew out of the sack three sandwiches, each carefully wrapped in wax paper, followed by three little glass bottles of mineral water. "Okay, boys and girls," he announced. "Lunchtime."

While they ate the lunch Pindar had brought, Joe learned the history of Learning Systems for Children and its founder, Nicole Martin.

Nicole had been a talented grade school teacher. The parents loved her approach to teaching, and her students loved *her*. But Nicole wasn't happy. She felt constrained by a system that was geared to teaching children only how to memorize and recite.

Over time, she devised a series of games that engaged the kids' creativity and intellectual curiosity. She was thrilled to find that her inventions helped the children learn and grow. But she grew frustrated with the fact that she couldn't help more than twenty or twenty-five kids at a time. And she was barely surviving on her teacher's salary.

"I expect you already know the First Law of Stratospheric Success?" she asked Joe.

"*Your true worth is determined by how much more you give in value than you take in payment,*" Joe replied.

"Very good," she said. "Gold star! But doing that doesn't necessarily mean that the *payment* you receive will increase."

Joe was relieved to hear her say this. He'd thought the same thing the day before, when he first heard Ernesto explain this Law.

"The First Law determines how *valuable* you are," Nicole continued. "In other words, your *potential* income, how much you *could* earn. But it's the Second Law that determines how much you actually *do* earn."

One day, while in conference with a parent, Nicole had mentioned how much the kids enjoyed the games she'd created and how much they seemed to benefit from them. Knowing this dad was a software engineer, she asked if she could hire him to take a look at them to see if it would be possible to program them to run on computers. He agreed.

The next week, Nicole met with the software designer again, and this time she brought along a school mom who ran a small marketing and advertising business. A few days later, the three formed a company together.

Nicole managed to find some seed capital through a friend of a friend, a man she simply called "the Connector." ("There's that 'Connector' again!" thought Joe. He would have to remember to ask Pindar about that.) Within a few years, their fledgling educational software company was doing over two hundred million dollars in annual sales worldwide. As founder and CEO of Learning Systems for Children, Inc., Nicole also did consulting for school systems, homeschooling organizations and educational researchers around the country.

"Through LSC, we expect to touch the lives of twenty to

twenty-five *million* kids," she pointed out. "And that in a nut-shell is the Second Law, the Law of Compensation:

> *"Your income is determined by*
> *how many people you serve*
> *and how well you serve them."*

She paused, then added, "Or to put it another way, *Your compensation is directly proportional to how many lives you touch.*"

Nicole sat and quietly finished her sandwich, giving Joe a chance to let the Law of Compensation sink in. After a brief silence, he began thinking out loud.

"You know, I always thought it seemed so unfair," he began, "how movie stars and top athletes pulled down those huge salaries. Or how CEOs and corporate founders could marshal such gigantic earnings. No offense," he added hastily.

She graciously nodded and gestured for him to go on.

"But people who were doing such great work, such noble work—like schoolteachers—never got paid what they're worth. It always seemed arbitrary. But what you're saying is, it's not just a question of their *value*. It's a question of *impact*."

Nicole and Pindar exchanged brief exultant glances, delighted at how quickly Joe had grasped this Law.

"Exactly," exclaimed Nicole. "And there are two amazing things about this. First, it means that you get to determine your level of compensation—it's under your control. If you want more success, find a way to serve more people. It's that simple."

Joe thought that over for a moment, then nodded. "And the other amazing thing?"

"It also means there are *no limitations* on what you can earn, because you can *always* find more people to serve. The Reverend Martin Luther King, Jr., once said, 'Everybody can be great because anybody can serve.' Another way to say that might be, 'Everybody can be successful because anybody can *give.*'"

Pindar was watching Joe closely. Now he spoke up. "You have a question."

Joe nodded. He asked Nicole, "I'm curious about that first meeting, the one with the software dad and the marketing mom? Didn't it occur to you that they might just take your ideas and run with them?"

Nicole looked puzzled. "Run with them?"

"I mean, steal them? Run with the whole idea and cut you out of the picture?"

Nicole smiled. "To tell you the truth, I never gave it a thought. All I could think about was how much good we could accomplish." She looked pensive, then gave a rueful laugh. "But I did go through an interesting period of adjustment. And that's when I really started to understand the Law of Compensation.

"Once I realized just how big this could grow, I nearly sabotaged the whole thing. Suddenly, it all made me nervous."

"Why? Were you afraid it would get out of hand and fall apart?"

She laughed. "No, quite the opposite. I was afraid it would get out of hand and become *really successful.*

"I was brought up with a belief that there are two types of people in the world. There are people who *get rich*, and there are people who *do good*. My belief system said you're one or the other, you can't be both.

"The people who got rich did so by taking advantage of everyone else. The people who really cared about others and provided services—policemen, nurses, volunteer workers and, of course, teachers—those were the world's *good* people, and they could never be rich. That would be a contradiction in terms.

"At least, that's what I grew up believing."

Joe was fascinated. "So what happened?"

"I watched how hard my partners were working. I saw how many kids' lives we were changing. And I saw that my old belief system was only getting in the way. It wasn't *serving*. So I decided to change it."

"You just decided?" asked Joe.

"Yup. Decided."

"So, you can just do that?" Joe said.

"Anyone can." She smiled, noting Joe's doubting look. "Have you ever made up a story?"

Joe glanced around the playroom/conference room. He flashed back to his kindergarten days and laughed. "I sure used to. Plenty of them."

"Your life works the same way," she said. "You just make it up. *Being broke and being rich are both decisions.* You make them up, right up here." She tapped her finger to her temple. "Everything else is just how it plays out."

Joe thought back to his Saturday morning conversation with Pindar. *What you focus on is what you get.*

All at once Joe heard a big *Whoop!* coming from the conference room next door, followed by a resounding cheer that broke into scattered laughter and applause.

Nicole smiled. "I think we just found our new Asia-Pacific marketing plan."

Pindar was on his feet, picking up the wrappers and bottles from their lunch, and before he knew it, Joe was shaking hands with Nicole and thanking her for her time.

"What's on your agenda for tomorrow, Joe?"

Joe looked inquiringly toward Pindar.

"Tomorrow we're going to visit Sam," he said.

"Ahh," said Nicole, "you're going to love Sam."

"Sam is Nicole's chief financial adviser," explained Pindar. "Mine, too."

As Pindar gave Nicole a hug and said his good-byes, Joe glanced around the room. He looked at the easels and finger paints, the clay and construction paper and all the other kindergarten paraphernalia, and a thought struck him.

"They make up stories," he mused to himself. "They sit here in this room and make up stories. They paint them and model them, and then go make them happen all over the planet—two hundred million dollars' worth!"

You just make it up, she'd said.

The Second Law

THE LAW OF COMPENSATION

*Your income is determined by
how many people you serve
and how well you serve them.*

6: Serving Coffee

The ride out of town was quiet. A friend of Pindar's had dropped him off at Learning Systems for Children earlier, so Joe was now giving him a ride back home. Pindar seemed content to watch the scenery go by, leaving Joe to his own thoughts.

Just as he had done after his lunch with Ernesto, Joe now retraced his conversation with Nicole Martin, trying to understand everything he'd heard.

What made this young woman rise to such astonishing success? Was it as simple as what she called the Law of Compensation?

When Joe pulled into Pindar's driveway to drop off his host, Rachel was standing at the front door, holding a small package. Pindar hopped out and Joe leaned over to call out to Rachel through the open door.

"Great lunch, Rachel. Thanks a million!"

Rachel approached the car and handed the package to Joe. "You're welcome."

The aroma announced itself immediately. It was a pound of Rachel's famous coffee, freshly ground for Joe.

On his drive back to work, Joe thought about Nicole

Martin, CEO of the kindergarten boardroom, and wondered how on earth he could possibly apply the Law of Compensation. He was still wrestling with these thoughts when he hit the UP button on the elevator that took him to the seventh floor at Clason-Hill Trust.

That afternoon, Melanie Matthews sat buried in concentration over her quarter-end reports when she was surprised by the most delicious aroma. She looked up and was startled to see Joe with a cup of fresh, steaming coffee for her.

"Touch of half-and-half, one sugar," he noted aloud as he placed it carefully on her desk.

This was exactly how Melanie liked her coffee, though she couldn't remember having ever mentioned this to Joe. And that incredible aroma! She thanked him and took a sip.

It was the very best coffee she had ever tasted.

Over the next thirty minutes, Joe took a cup of the hot, delicious coffee to each worker on the entire seventh floor. A few of them he knew well, some he knew only vaguely, some he'd never even met. All were equally surprised and pleased to find this young go-getter taking the time to serve them fresh coffee as they each wrestled with their own third-quarter-deadline workloads. One or two looked downright puzzled as they nodded their mute thanks, thinking, "Wonder what's gotten into *him*?"

When Joe arrived back at his own desk with the last cup, Gus sat waiting for him.

"Gus, you want another cup?"

"Thanks, but I'm fine." Gus sat back in his chair and looked at Joe with curiosity.

"Okay," said Joe, "you know the guy I asked you about last week? Pindar? Well, this weekend, I went to see him."

"Ah," said Gus, "and this is what, something like home-work?"

Joe shrugged. "More or less. Yesterday, I had to 'give more in value than I got in payment.'"

"Ah. The lead you gave to Jim Galloway."

Joe blushed. So Gus *had* overheard him doing that. "To-day, I had to 'enlarge the number of people I serve.'"

Gus let out a quiet laugh. "So you served your colleagues coffee."

"Right." Joe looked around the floor. "Think it'll turn those third-quarter figures around?"

Gus peered at him closely, then realized he was joking.

"Hey," Joe added, "it's the only thing I could think of. Besides, it's not just coffee. It's Rachel's *famous* coffee."

Gus smiled and got to his feet. "I'm glad you went to see the man, Joe. Tell me something."

"Sure, what?"

Gus looked around the office. "How did it feel, serving all those people?"

Joe followed his gaze, then looked back in the other man's eyes. "Tell you the truth? I felt like an idiot."

Gus laughed again, then leaned forward and said:

"Sometimes you feel foolish, even look foolish, but you do the thing anyway."

And with that, he plucked his tweed jacket from the coat-rack on the wall outside his office and headed for home.

7: Rachel

When Joe appeared at Pindar's house at noon the next day, Rachel showed him into the study and offered him a cup of coffee, which Joe accepted gratefully.

"The Old Man'll be right along," Rachel said, and chuckled.

"You know," said Joe, "I think that's the third or fourth time I've heard that. 'The Old Man.' Why does everyone keep calling him that? And what's the big joke?"

Rachel set down the small tray she was carrying and leaned against one of the huge wingback chairs. "How old would you say he is?" she asked.

"Gosh, I don't know, fifty-eight, fifty-nine? Early sixties maybe?"

"Close." Rachel grinned. "Seventy-eight."

"You're kidding!" exclaimed Joe.

"And even though he's in his late seventies, he's one of the *youngest* people I know. Have you noticed how energetic and enthusiastic he is? How curious and . . . well, how *interested* he always seems?"

Joe nodded.

"I'll tell you what," Rachel went on, "he does more, travels more and accomplishes more than most men half his age. None of us can keep up with him."

"Really!" Pindar didn't strike Joe as the driven type. "But he always seems so . . . relaxed."

Rachel laughed. "Of course he seems relaxed. He *is* relaxed. Whoever said being anxious gets more accomplished?"

Joe had to admit she had a point. He had always taken it for granted that getting a lot done invariably meant a high level of stress. But then, he knew plenty of people who were thoroughly stressed out, yet didn't really accomplish that much.

"Who are you going to see today?" Rachel asked.

"Sam. His financial adviser."

"Ahh, Sam." Rachel smiled to herself. "You're going to love Sam."

"So I've heard," thought Joe.

"Of course he will." Pindar stood beaming at the study door. "Everyone loves Sam!"

The moment he heard that storyteller's voice, Joe felt himself relax. He noticed it had the same effect on Rachel, too. He suspected it had that effect on *everyone*.

As Joe nosed his car past the big wrought-iron gates and pointed it toward downtown, he thought about his brief conversation with Rachel, and he asked Pindar about her.

Rachel came from a poor neighborhood and began working to help support her family when she was just fifteen years old. She took work doing anything and everything. She cleaned houses, landscaped, answered phones, waited tables, short-order cooked, worked construction, painted houses, and more. Eventually, she put herself through college on this diverse collection of jobs.

Some of these tasks she enjoyed more than others. However, she approached each one as though she *loved* it. She did this by reminding herself that, regardless of how much or how little she cared for the task itself, she relished the opportunity to *survive, save and serve.*

"Survive, save and serve?" Joe interrupted. "Sounds like a motto."

"It easily could be," agreed Pindar. "They are the three universal reasons for working. *Survive*—to meet your basic living needs. *Save*—to go beyond your basic needs and expand your life. *And serve*—to make a contribution to the world around you."

Joe thought of Nicole Martin's reflection on her own early fear of success. *It wasn't serving*, she'd said.

"Unfortunately," continued Pindar, "most people spend their entire lives focusing on the first. A smaller number focus on the second. But those rare few who are truly successful— not just financially, but *genuinely* successful in all aspects of their lives—keep their focus squarely on the third."

Survive, save and serve. Joe let the three words roll around in his mind as Pindar continued the story of Rachel.

About a year ago, Pindar had bought some books at a local bookseller's where Rachel had worked her way up to café manager. After making his purchase, he stopped by the café for a cup of coffee.

"I'm just starting a fresh pot," Rachel told him. "If you're not in a hurry, why don't you make yourself comfortable on any of the reading sofas, and I'll bring you a cup as soon as it's ready."

Pindar was impressed with the young woman's manner. He was even more impressed when he actually tasted the coffee.

Rachel had an undeniable knack for making truly wonderful coffee. She had an instinct for selecting, blending, roasting and grinding the beans to bring out their finest flavors and aromas. She had a master craftsman's feel for the perfect balance of time and temperature. She knew how to keep the machines sparkling clean and free of any buildup of bitter oils, and how to select the purest sources of water. Her coffee *always* tasted delicious—better than delicious.

"Whenever people ask her for her secret," Pindar told Joe, "she just laughs and says she's one-eighth Colombian."

Pindar and his wife happened to be looking for someone to replace their personal chef, who had just been offered a position running the kitchen at a five-star hotel. As far as Pindar was concerned, anyone who knew how to cook and could make coffee this good would be the perfect replacement. And since she had just completed her final term at college, she was available.

He hired Rachel on the spot.

The young woman quickly became a hit with the steady stream of business associates who passed through Pindar's home, including the CEOs of some of the nation's largest companies. A few even hinted that they might try to hire Rachel away from Pindar, but he jokingly warned them that if they even tried, they would no longer be privy to his consulting services. One CEO, after hearing this, took a long, thoughtful sip of "famous" coffee and murmured, "Yes, well . . . I might just have to live with that."

Pindar roared at this punch line, and Joe laughed along with him. He also had the sense that there was more to Rachel's story, but it would have to wait. They had arrived at their destination.

8: The Law of Influence

Perched on the top floors of the city's tallest and most elegant office building, the regional headquarters of the Liberty Life Insurance and Financial Services Company was located right in the heart of the financial district.

Most of the building's twenty-four floors were rented to the city's top investment companies and law firms. The twenty-second and twenty-third were occupied by Liberty. Sam's offices, where Joe and Pindar were headed, took up the entire twenty-fourth floor.

Inside the front door, Pindar signed them in with the security guard. They passed through a beautifully appointed lobby and entered a tall glass elevator framed with exquisite filigree and floored with plush, royal blue carpeting.

"They must sell a lot of policies," whispered Joe.

"This is the single most successful branch office of the single most successful financial services company in the world," Pindar whispered back. "You're about to meet the person who single-handedly accounts for more than three quarters of all the money this particular branch brings in."

"You must be Joe!" The beaming, white-haired gentleman grabbed Joe's hand with both of his own and shook it vigorously. His voice sounded like a creaky gate hinge. "It's about time the Old Man brought someone around I could have some fun talking to. He's boring!" And he thumped Pindar on the shoulder.

As Sam wheezed with laughter and led his guests to two sumptuous leather chairs, Joe glanced around the place. The vast twenty-fourth-floor work space looked more like an airplane hangar than a corporate office. The vaulted ceiling and huge skylights were at least twenty feet overhead. Through the two huge plate glass walls that formed the corner office's perimeter Joe could see that amazing western mountain landscape beyond the city.

Joe tore himself away from the view to focus on the conversation as Pindar and Sam ping-ponged through a brief history of Sam's career.

Sam Rosen had started out as a struggling insurance agent. Over the years, he gained a reputation as an especially fairminded businessman. People started calling on him to serve as a negotiator or, in their more difficult dealings, as a mediator. After establishing himself as the firm's top salesman, he broadened his focus and began serving as a full-spectrum financial adviser for select clients.

In his early sixties, Sam shifted gears yet again. He began to work with nonprofits, especially those helping the financially disadvantaged, the homeless and the hungry. Today Sam was the state's number one philanthropist and spent most of his time negotiating large contracts on behalf of worldwide charities.

"When I first met him a little over thirty years ago," added Pindar, "he had already amassed over four hundred million dollars in sales—more by far than anyone else in the history of his company."

"You must be the best insurance salesman in the world," ventured Joe.

"Should be, should be," Sam agreed. "I started out as the worst! When my goal was to sell insurance, I was no good at all. My first few years in the business, I floundered like a turtle on his back. Tell you what it was turned things around and set me right side up—"

Joe held up one finger and said, "May I guess? The idea of *giving more in value than you took in payment*?"

"Not a bad guess," said Sam. "Changing my focus from seeing what I could *git* to what I could *give* was when my career started to take off. *Started* to. But in a business like mine— actually, in *any* business—you also need to know how to *develop a network*."

He looked directly at Joe. "Do you know what I mean by 'network'?"

In fact, Joe had just been thinking that networking was something he indeed knew all about, but the question caught him by surprise and he quickly shook his head. "No—I mean, yes, I think I do." He paused. "But I'll bet I don't," he finished lamely.

Sam's eyes twinkled with warmth. "The Old Man was right again, as usual. He said I'd like you."

Joe blushed.

Sam continued. "Now, by a *network* I don't necessarily mean your customers or clients. I mean a network of people who *know you, like you and trust you.* They might never buy a thing from you, but they've always got you in the backs of their minds." He leaned forward and spoke with more intensity. "They're people who are personally invested in seeing you succeed, y'see? And of course, that's because you're the same way about them. They're your army of *personal walking ambassadors.*

"When you've got your own army of *personal walking ambassadors,* you'll have referrals coming your way faster than you can handle them."

Joe had always considered himself an accomplished networker, but he now found himself reexamining every business contact and networking relationship he had. *An army of personal walking ambassadors.* Did that describe *his* network? Were all these people he knew "personally invested in seeing him succeed"?

Did that description fit *any* of them?

Sam spoke again, in a quiet voice this time. "You want to know what makes that kind of network happen, Joe?"

Joe looked up and met Sam's gaze. "I do."

The old man's eyes bore into Joe. "*Stop keeping score.*"

Joe blinked. "How—how do you mean?"

Sam settled back into his chair. "Just that. Don't keep track. That's not networking—that's poker. You know how people say 'win-win'?"

Joe nodded. "Always look for the solution where you both come out ahead."

Sam nodded. "That's right, and it sounds great—in theory. But most of the time, what people call 'win-win' is really just a disguised way of keeping track. Making sure we all come out even, that nobody gets the advantage. Even-Steven. I scratched your back, so now you owe me." He shook his head sadly. "When you base your relationships—in business or anywhere else in your life—on who owes who what, that's not being a *friend*. That's being a *creditor*."

Joe remembered what he'd said last Friday on the phone: "C'mon, Carl, you owe me one! Hey, who saved your bacon on the Hodges account?"

Sam leaned forward again. "You want to know the Third Law of Stratospheric Success?"

Joe nodded. "Very much indeed."

"*Watch out for the other guy*. Watch out for *his* interests. Watch *his* back. Forget about fifty-fifty, son. Fifty-fifty's a losing proposition. *The only winning proposition is one hundred percent*. Make your win about the other person, go after what *he* wants. Forget win-win—*focus on the other person's win*.

"Here it is, Joe. The Third Law, the Law of Influence:

> *"Your influence is determined by*
> *how abundantly you place*
> *other people's interests first."*

Joe repeated it slowly. "Your influence is determined by how abundantly you place other people's interests first."

Sam nodded, beaming.

Joe hesitated, glanced at Pindar, then back at Sam. "That sounds like an awfully noble principle," he began, "but I don't quite understand . . ."

Sam peered at him. "Don't quite git how that's a law of *success?*"

Relieved, Joe nodded. "Exactly."

Sam looked over at Pindar and nodded toward Joe, as if to say, *You tell him.*

Pindar spoke up. "Because if you place the other person's interests first, *your* interests will always be taken care of. *Always.* Some people call it *enlightened self-interest.* Watch out for what other people need, with the faith that when you do, you'll get what *you* need."

Sam nodded and watched Joe grapple with this idea for a moment, then said, "Tell me, if you asked most people what creates influence, what would they say?"

Joe's answer came without hesitation. "Money. Position. Maybe a history of outstanding accomplishments."

Sam nodded, grinning. "Ha! You're right, that's *exactly* what they'd say—and they'd have it exactly backwards! Those things don't *create* influence—influence creates *them.*

"And now you know what creates *it.*"

Joe blinked. "Putting other people's interests first?"

Sam's smile was beatific. "Now you're talkin'."

Joe followed Pindar into the elevator. Side by side, they watched the doors close. As they began their descent, Pindar broke the silence. "How would you describe Sam?"

"Amazing. Brilliant. Magnetic."

"Mmm. *Magnetic*." Pindar seemed to ponder the word. "What about Nicole? Would you describe her as *magnetic*?"

"Absolutely. One of the most striking people I've ever met."

Pindar looked at Joe and said, "Tell me, what is it about her that makes her so?"

Joe had to think about that. What *was* it that made her so striking? "I don't know, she's just . . . *magnetic*."

Pindar smiled. "Like Sam?"

It was hard to imagine two more different people than the charming young schoolteacher and the raspy old financier— but yes, they were somehow very much alike. And not just them . . . "Yes! And Ernesto, too, and—" He was going to say, "And you, too!" but stopped short. He stared at Pindar. "What is it? You know, don't you?"

Bing! They had reached the ground floor. The doors slid open and Pindar gestured with his hand: *After you.* As they walked through the marble, steel and glass of the building's majestic foyer, Pindar uttered a single word:

"Giving."

"Huh? What about giving?"

"That's what they have in common. Giving." He glanced sideways at Joe and smiled. "Have you ever wondered what makes people attractive? I mean, genuinely attractive? Magnetic?" He pushed on the big glass door and they walked outdoors into the warm September day. "They love to give. That's why they're attractive. *Givers attract*."

They walked silently toward his car. "Givers attract," thought Joe. "And that's why the Law of Influence works. Because it *magnetizes* you."

The Third Law

THE LAW OF INFLUENCE

*Your influence is determined by
how abundantly you place
other people's interests first.*

9: Susan

When Joe returned to his office that afternoon, things were in chaos. Their computer system had gone down for a few minutes, and in the process of getting it back online, three days of account records and correspondence had been lost. Everyone was frantically pulling files and restoring information to the system from hard copies.

As Joe joined his team and plowed into the growing stack of papers, all thoughts of Sam Rosen, Pindar and the Law of Influence evaporated.

It was nearly seven when he finally closed his paper-stuffed briefcase, picked it up with a groan and headed for the elevator.

He dropped into the seat of his car, his mind still churning on his work. The next thing he knew, he was pulling into his driveway twenty-five minutes later.

He switched off the engine and sat listening to the *clink-clink-clink* of the cooling engine. He wished there were an ignition key that would switch off his mind. Was he wasting his time with these daily lunchtime lessons and Laws of

Stratospheric Success he was supposedly learning? Was any of this getting him closer to making that third-quarter quota he so badly needed to make?

He looked at the front door of his suburban duplex and sighed.

Susan would have been home for an hour already. She would be just as exhausted as he was, and her afternoon would have been just as hard as his.

He found Susan in the kitchen, pulling something from the oven. She didn't need to tell him that he was late or that their dinner was a little dried out. Or that she was too tired to care one way or the other. Her body language said all that and more.

Over a listless dinner, notes were compared and miseries tallied as the two moved through the meal and kitchen cleanup. Joe wanted to tell her all about his appointment at the imposing Liberty office building, but he gave up without even trying.

Last Saturday, when Joe had returned home and told her his first impressions of Pindar, Susan had been intrigued. But at dinner on Monday, when he tried to tell her about Ernesto, she said only, "So this guy is actually the owner?" She repeated this a few times and couldn't seem to get any deeper into his story. Yesterday, when he started telling her about Nicole Martin's kindergarten conference room, she rolled her eyes and said, "You're kidding." It went no further.

Joe and Susan had established a sort of unwritten rule. They both had high-stress jobs and would arrive home for the evening in knots, each with at least a solid hour or two of extra office work to do. The unwritten rule was this: "We each get up to thirty minutes of complaint time, no more."

Tonight, Susan was already well into her half hour. Joe sat on the edge of their bed, doing his best to stay sympathetic while Susan paced and talked. Inwardly he sighed again, wondering what he could possibly say that would make her feel better.

Suddenly Joe realized that Susan had stopped talking mid-sentence and was looking at him.

"I'm sorry," she said softly. "It's almost eight thirty . . ." A tired sigh. "I guess I'm a bottomless pity party." A wan attempt at a smile. "I know you've got work to get to." She turned away and said, more to herself than to him, "Fair's fair."

Joe opened his mouth to speak, then closed it again.

Fair's fair. What did that remind him of? And why did it sound so . . . wrong? *Fifty-fifty's a losing proposition.* It was Sam, of course. *Even-Steven. I scratched your back, so now you owe me . . . that's not being a friend, that's being a credito*r. Was that what their marriage had become?

Without thinking about what he was going to say, he blurted out, "No, Suse, wait. Actually, I don't."

She turned back and looked at him.

"Please, go on," he said. "I'd like to hear about what happened. Really."

For a moment, Susan looked at Joe as if he had told her that the laws of gravity had just been revoked. "Really?"

"Sure," he said. "I mean, it sounds like it was pretty rough. So what did you do?"

His wife sat next to him on the bed and looked at him again.

"Really," he said. "My stuff will wait."

Susan slowly began to talk again about her day, about an especially nasty conflict she was having with a coworker. After a few minutes she stopped mid-sentence again and looked at Joe.

He nodded and waited for her to go on.

She lay back against the pillow and began to pour her heart out. She talked about how long this difficult situation at work had been brewing, why it hurt her so, how lost she was as to what to do about it. How it made her feel.

Twenty minutes later, she was crying.

Joe was mortified. He'd been listening carefully, but she'd talked about so many different issues and covered so much ground, he wasn't sure exactly which thing she was crying about. It seemed as if for Susan, *everything* was wrong.

He lay down and put his arm around her awkwardly, but her weeping continued. He murmured a few attempts at words of comfort, feeling foolish all the while.

What was it Gus had said? *Sometimes you feel foolish, even look foolish, but you do the thing anyway. . . .*

Finally, her sobbing turned to sniffling, and then that stopped, too.

Joe felt immense relief. Perhaps his words were not so foolish after all. They seemed to have given her some comfort, at least. Or perhaps she was just thinking.

"Hey," he said. "Love you."

Susan said nothing.

"Suse?" He stirred her gently.

She was asleep. She hadn't heard any of his words of comfort—she'd just cried herself to sleep.

Feeling useless and defeated, Joe quietly got himself ready for bed and slipped under the covers. Wrapped in a quiet ache for Susan's misery and wishing he could have done something to take away its sting, he eventually drifted off.

The next morning he awoke with a start and lurched from deep sleep into sudden horrified realization: yesterday's lesson! What was it? Sam Rosen . . . networking . . . *an army of personal walking ambassadors.*

The Law of Influence.

He had gone from work to home to bed and passed the night away without even *thinking* about the day's lesson, let alone trying to apply it.

He groaned and grabbed his pillow, meaning to throw it across the room in frustration, but as he did, he realized that Susan was not in the bed next to him. He glanced at the clock. Eight fifteen. He had overslept! Susan must have crept out of bed and left the house without talking to him, without even bothering to wake him.

He groaned again. He'd blown Pindar's lesson, he was late for work and he was on the outs with Susan. "Three strikes, Joe," he muttered.

Pindar's words echoed in his mind. "If you don't abide by my Condition, our meetings will come to an end."

He dragged himself upright, with sinking thoughts about calling Brenda to cancel his lunch appointment with Pindar.

And then he glanced at Susan's pillow and noticed a piece of paper, folded in half, with a single word written on the outside:

Sweetheart—

When was the last time Susan had called him that? Come to think of it, when was the last time Susan had written him a note? He picked it up and opened it.

My Sweet Joe—

I hope I succeeded in slipping out without waking you. You deserve the extra rest! After the earful I gave you last night . . .

Thank you so much.

Thank you for your generosity.

Generosity? "My Sweet Joe"? He read the rest of the note.

I can't remember ever feeling so . . . so <u>listened to</u>. So <u>heard</u>.

I love you.

—S.

Joe was at a loss. Generosity? What had he been generous about? He looked back at the note, scanning it for answers.

Thank you for your generosity.

I can't remember ever feeling so . . . so <u>listened to</u>.

He rubbed his face, amazed. It wasn't about complaining at all. She just wanted him to *listen*. Just wanted to be *heard*.

All at once he remembered that voice like a creaking gate hinge—*Stop keeping score!*—and then he laughed.

He *had* done the homework!

10: The Law of Authenticity

"What was it like?" They were the first words either had spoken the whole fifteen minutes they'd been on the road into town.

Much like yesterday, when he'd been unable to stop thinking about the office, Joe was now having a hard time tearing his mind away from Susan's note and her tearful aria of woes the night before. Pindar's query caught him off guard.

"Sir?" Joe didn't think he'd called Pindar "Sir" since their first meeting.

"Applying the Third Law," said Pindar. "What was that like for you?"

It occurred to Joe that up to this point, Pindar had never once asked him anything about his "homework" or checked to make sure he was fulfilling the Condition.

So why was he asking now? A glance at Pindar told him the man wasn't checking up on him. He was asking because he genuinely wanted to know. "It's because he knows something happened," he thought. "Something important."

"It was . . . it went okay. I mean, I think it did. Honestly, I'm not sure."

Pindar nodded, as if Joe's response made complete sense. "These lessons don't apply only to business, Joe. A genuinely sound business principle will apply anywhere in life—in your friendships, in your marriage, *anywhere*. That's the true bottom line. Not whether it simply improves your financial balance sheet, but whether it improves your *life's* balance sheet."

"I guess I never thought about that before."

"I highly recommend it." He glanced sideways at Joe. "My wife and I, remember, have been married for nearly fifty years."

"Fifty years," Joe echoed. *Fifty years*. The man's marriage had lasted nearly twice Joe's current lifespan.

"Now, this is going to sound very old-fashioned." Pindar glanced at Joe again, as if looking for confirmation that Joe understood this.

"Okay," Joe said, nodding.

"I believe there is one reason, and only one reason, that we have stayed together so long and are as happy together today as we were forty-eight years ago—more so, in fact. That reason is this: *I care more about my wife's happiness than I do about my own*. All I've ever wanted to do since the day I met her is make her happy. And here's the truly remarkable thing—she seems to want the same thing for me."

"Wouldn't some people call that codependent?" ventured Joe.

"Yes, some probably would. Know what I call it?"

"Happy?"

Pindar laughed. "Yes, certainly that. I was going to say, I'd call that *success*."

Success. Joe thought about his life with Susan and how it had begun to feel like a constant drama of battle and compromise. *Fifty-fifty's a losing proposition. . . .*

"Like what Sam says about networking," he commented.

"Exactly." Pindar pointed out the windshield. "And here we are."

Joe saw the huge auditorium looming ahead and turned in to the underground parking lot.

They were going to hear the keynote speaker at an annual sales symposium. It was one of the city's largest events, and it attracted participants from all over the country. Today's speaker, though, was a local resident. Her name was Debra Davenport.

The place was packed, but Pindar had reserved two seats for them at the back of the large hall. Joe was impressed by the size of the crowd. He guessed there were a good three thousand people waiting to hear the speaker.

And she did not disappoint. After the symposium's master of ceremonies gave a brief, glowing introduction, the speaker stepped center stage to a standing ovation from the crowd. She waited gracefully until they had finished their applause and seated themselves.

"Twelve years ago I turned forty-two," she began. "I got three presents for my birthday.

"One. My best friend gave me a hundred-dollar gift certificate to JCPenney, which in those days was the high-water mark of my fashion existence." She paused, looked to the right and to the left, then leaned forward toward the audience and struck a confidential, just-between-you-and-me pose. "And by the way," she added, "JCPenney is *still* my number one fashion experience."

This was greeted by a round of laughter and applause. She grinned and waved everyone quiet.

"I mean, why throw your money away on overpriced fashion that'll just be obsolete next year? Am I right? Besides, ladies?" She tapped her index finger a few times to her temple. "It's what's inside that makes you beautiful, not the wrapping."

Another wave of laughter and applause rushed through the place. "We're sixty seconds in, and she *owns* the room," Joe marveled to himself.

Debra Davenport continued.

"Two. My three kids pooled their money and got their mom an all-day, all-expenses-paid retreat at a spa downtown. I mean, the expensive kind. All day! And they planned it so they had enough left over to pay the babysitter. In fact"—for just a breath, she wavered and seemed about to cry—"in fact, they had called her and set it up so that she'd be there all day *without* my finding out ahead of time. Which, knowing how nosy their mom can be, was a miracle of administrative genius and first-rate sneakiness."

The crowd laughed a warm rustle of appreciation.

"Three. My husband gave me the most surprising gift of all. He gave me the wake-up call of a lifetime—when he walked out the door and never came back."

Joe felt the room take a breath and hold it.

"It took me one full year to unwrap, open, understand and use that gift."

She looked around, and Joe saw that she was meeting the eyes of individual after individual, not only in the first few rows, but throughout the crowded auditorium.

"Today, I want to share that gift with every one of you."

For the next fifteen minutes, the speaker took them through her story.

At forty-two, suddenly single and with three kids to feed, Debra had never spent a day in the mainstream workforce. As a full-time mother, wife and manager of a busy household, she had juggled dozens of skills and worked grueling hours. But as she quickly learned, none of what she'd spent the last twenty-odd years doing was considered marketable.

"Everywhere I applied," she told the audience, "I was overage and under-qualified."

After her husband left town, she spent the next few months pursuing a real estate license. Debra was a quick study and passed the exam on her first try. The following eight or nine months were busy with learning and trying to follow all the advice and teaching of those in her firm.

"They taught me every kind of sales methodology and closing technique ever invented. I learned the Direct Close, the Deal/Concession Close, the Time-Driven Close and the Trial Offer Close. They taught me the Compliment Close and the Embarrassment Close, the Best-Time-to-Buy Close and the Never-the-Best-Time-to-Buy Close, the Courtship Close and the Shame Close. I learned every close from A to Z."

She paused, looked around, then deadpanned, "Oh, you don't believe me." A ripple of laughter went through the first few rows. Joe guessed there were some Debra Davenport fans who already knew whatever riff might be coming next.

"Well, let's see . . ." she began, then started counting them on her fingers. "There was the Assumptive Close, the Bonus Close, the Concession Close, the Distraction Close, the Emotion Close, the Future Close . . ."—the people in the first row began to clap in rhythm, one clap to each new letter of the alphabet—". . . the Golden Gate Bridge Close, the Humor Close, the IQ Close, the Jersey City Close . . ."—and now the whole audience joined in, marking each beat with a loud *clap!*—". . . the Kill Clause Close, the Leveraged Asset Close, the Money's-Not-Everything Close, the Now-or-Never Close, the Ownership Close, the Puppy Dog Close, the Quality Close, the Reversal Close, the Standing-Room-Only Close, the Takeaway Close, the Underpriced-Value Close, the Vanity Close, the Window-of-Opportunity Close . . ."—and she took a big breath—". . . the Xaviera Hollander Close, the Ya-Ya Sisterhood Close and the Zsa Zsa Gabor Close!

"Honey, I learned how to *close*!"

The rhythmic clapping dissolved into a huge round of applause as everyone laughed and cheered her bravura performance. She held her hands up, eyes twinkling, until the laughter and clapping died down.

"And let me tell you what happened. At the end of a year, I had not sold one, single, solitary property. And I hated it. Every single, desperate, failing minute of it."

The hall was silent.

"That Thursday, I turned forty-three. For this birthday, my best friend bought me a ticket to a sales symposium. Tell you the truth, I didn't want to go. But she was my best friend." She smiled. "Still is, by the way," and she beamed down at the front row, where Joe guessed the woman in question was seated. "So what could I do? She's awfully persuasive." Laughter from a cluster of women in front confirmed Joe's guess.

"I went to the symposium." She looked around, as if suddenly recognizing where she was for the first time. "Actually, it was *this* symposium. Matter of fact, I sat right where you are all sitting right now, on a Thursday afternoon in September just like this one.

"That year, the keynote speaker was a man I'd never heard of before. He talked about the importance of adding value to what you sell. 'Whatever it is you sell,' he told us, 'even if it's a mundane commodity that everyone else is selling, too, whether it's real estate, insurance or hot dogs,'" and with a chill, Joe realized that Ms. Davenport was talking about the man sitting next to him, "'whatever it is,' he said, *'you can excel by adding value*. If you need money,' he said, 'add value. And if you need a *lot* of money, add a *lot* of value.'

"People in the audience laughed when he said that, but I didn't see anything funny. I was sitting way in the back, feeling just awful about my life. Somehow I got up the courage to raise my hand. His eyes lit right on me, and he said, 'Yes? The woman in back?' And I stood up and said, 'What if you need a lot of money *fast*?' He nodded, smiled and said, 'Then find a way to add a lot of value *fast*!'"

The audience responded with a quiet ripple of laughter.

"Ladies and gentlemen, let me tell you, I thought about what he said all that weekend. I thought about it hard. What value could I possibly add to a real estate listing by a failed broker in a buyer's market?

"Sunday evening, it came to me. What could I possibly add? *Nothing*.

"There was not one, single, solitary shred or ounce of value I could think of that insignificant little Debra Davenport could add. After a year of trying, I'd proven I had no professional value whatsoever. What I had to offer these clients was *nothing*.

"That Sunday evening, I made up my mind. It was time to quit."

She paused. "I'd just—" She paused again, took a breath to steady her emotion. She tapped her finger on her temple again and looked out at the group.

"You understand what was going on, in here? When my husband walked out that door, my self-esteem got up and walked out with him."

Joe noticed hundreds of heads nodding. She was touching a powerful chord.

"My husband had seen me more as a liability than as an asset. The job market had agreed with him, and obviously so did the world of real estate. Who was I to argue the point?"

Joe glanced around and noticed quite a few damp pairs of eyes. What mysterious power did this woman hold over them?

Debra Davenport gave a slow, sad shake of her head.

"A year later, and I still hadn't unwrapped my birthday gift."

She took a sharp breath and let it out again, as if to shake off the mood.

"So, I went in the next morning ready to clean out my desk. I had one last appointment that I couldn't weasel out of, so purely out of obligation, I met the prospect and drove her to see the house. 'It's already over,' I told myself, 'so what the heck.' I just let myself have a good time with her. I let go of all the techniques. I didn't even bring spec sheets on the house!"

She clucked disapprovingly.

"On the way over, we just chattered, talked about everything and anything, silly stuff. I couldn't tell you for sure whether I ever even told her the asking price! It was the most unprofessional, sloppy, irresponsible, disgraceful sales presentation in the history of real estate."

She held up both hands in an attitude of exasperation, as if to say, *What a ditz, huh?*

"And, of course, she bought the house."

It took a full minute for the applause to die down enough for her to go on with her story.

"I learned something that day. When I said that my life as a mom, wife and household manager left me with nothing the marketplace wanted, I was wrong. There *was* something else I'd learned over those years, and that was how to be a friend. How to care. How to make people feel good about themselves. And that, my friends, is something the marketplace wants very much—always has, always will.

"The speaker at that symposium had said, *Add value.* I had nothing to add but myself.

"And, apparently, that was exactly what'd been missing."

She paused and took a deep breath, giving her feelings a moment to settle.

"I've sold a few more homes since then," she began, and an appreciative wave of laughter went through the audience. Everyone present knew Debra Davenport's sales record. "A few more homes" was probably the understatement of the decade.

"Later I met the husband of the woman I sold that first house to, and he connected me to some friends who were getting involved in commercial real estate. I'd said I would never do that. Wrong again!"

Debra Davenport's comment, "and he connected me to some friends," touched a loose thread in Joe's mind, something he'd meant to ask a few days earlier but had forgotten about until now. He leaned over to Pindar and whispered, "The Connector?"

Pindar smiled and nodded.

"Aha," thought Joe. So it was Debra Davenport who sold Ernesto the enterprising café owner his multimillion-dollar commercial properties! When would he get to meet this Connector character?

". . . and I've had the honor of being named this city's top Realtor in both residential and commercial markets . . ."

Joe's mind was still buzzing. If it was this Connector who had linked up Ernesto Iafrate and Debra Davenport, and had helped arrange the financing for Nicole Martin's fledgling software business . . . He leaned over again and whispered, "Who are we going to meet tomorrow?"

Pindar whispered, "Ah, the Friday Guest." He nodded to himself. "The Friday Guest is a surprise."

"It's the Connector, isn't it?" Joe asked. "I'm finally going to meet the Connector?"

Pindar just smiled and wouldn't say another word.

". . . and in the past few years," Debra Davenport was saying, "I've crisscrossed the country speaking to groups just like this group today, and I tell every one of them the same thing. I'm here because I have the awesome responsibility and honor of selling you something far more valuable than a house.

"What I'm here to sell you on is *you*.

"People, remember this: no matter what your training, no matter what your skills, no matter what area you're in, *you* are your most important commodity. The most valuable gift you have to offer is *you*.

"Reaching any goal you set takes ten percent specific knowledge or technical skills—ten percent, *max*. The other ninety-plus percent is *people* skills.

"And what's the foundation of all people skills? Liking people? Caring about people? Being a good listener? Those are all helpful, but they're not the core of it. The core of it is *who you are*. It starts with *you*.

"As long as you're trying to be someone else, or putting on some act or behavior someone else taught you, you have no possibility of truly reaching people. *The most valuable thing you have to give people is yourself.* No matter what you *think* you're selling, what you're really offering is *you.*"

She glanced toward the back of the hall—and Joe was startled to realize she was looking directly at him. Or at least, it certainly seemed like it to Joe.

"You want great people skills?" She leaned in toward the audience as if confiding something to her best friend.

"You want people skills?" she repeated. "Then be a *person.*" She looked around from face to face. "Can you do that? *Will* you do that?"

She looked to the left and to the right, again, meeting the gaze of dozens of individuals.

"It's worth ten thousand times more than all the closing techniques that ever have been or ever will be invented.

"It's called *authenticity.*"

Joe remembered wondering what mysterious power this woman held over them—and knew he had just heard the answer.

They pulled out of the parking garage in silence and threaded their way through the downtown maze. Joe had thought about many things in the last few days and had reevaluated much about the way he did business. But he had not been prepared for the impact that Debra Davenport had on him with that single word.

Authenticity.

He glanced over at Pindar's impassive expression, unreadable as the Sphinx, then back at the road.

"You know why I came to see you Saturday?"

Pindar nodded. "You were hungry to learn about success. Genuine success."

Joe paused, then said, "Actually . . . no. Not really. The truth is . . ."

Pindar glanced at him, his eyes serious. "Go on."

Joe took a breath. "I came to see you because I wanted to impress you. I wanted to gain your trust, and I was hoping—planning, actually—to persuade you to help me put this deal together. This deal I'm working on. To bring your money and connections and, you know . . ." Joe's voice dropped to an almost inaudible confession. "Your clout."

There it was. He'd said it, and now it was out in the open. His reason for coming to see the man in the first place. The BK account. *Clout and leverage.*

Joe had never seen Pindar angry. He certainly didn't want to see it now. Nevertheless, he took another breath, then forced himself to turn back and look his mentor in the eye.

"It was a stupid reason," Joe said.

Pindar spoke softly. "No, not stupid. It's where you were, that's all. Besides, that wasn't the reason you came to see me. You only *thought* it was the reason you came to see me."

Joe stared at him. "Then what *was* the real reason I came?"

Pindar smiled. "You were hungry to learn about success. Genuine success."

The Fourth Law

THE LAW OF AUTHENTICITY

*The most valuable gift you have to offer
is yourself.*

11: Gus

Gus left Joe alone that afternoon. He sensed the younger man needed some space. He didn't know exactly what had happened, but he suspected that Joe was experiencing the cleansing pain of honest self-reflection.

As five o'clock approached, Gus closed up his desk, switched off his lamp, gathered up his things and padded over to pluck his tweed jacket from the coatrack.

"Gus?"

He turned and saw Joe looking at him. "Mmm?" The young man looked pensive. No, it was more: he looked positively contrite.

"You have a minute?"

Gus left his jacket on the rack. "Sure." He took a seat next to Joe's desk, folded his hands and looked up.

Joe came around the desk, pulled a chair over and sat down next to Gus. "I need to tell you something." Joe paused.

Gus waited.

"You've been good to me, ever since I first got here. And I've always thought of you as . . . well, a little naïve. Old-fashioned. You know?"

Gus nodded.

"I never believed the rumors about you," said Joe. "I mean, the ones about them just keeping you on out of loyalty. And I never believed the other rumors, either, the ones about how successful you've been. But that part's true, isn't it? These Five Laws, all Pindar's stuff about giving, you *know* all this stuff, don't you?"

Gus regarded Joe for a moment before answering.

"I have been very fortunate in my career," he began. "And yes, I have been to the stone mansion and learned those same lessons you've been learning this week." Gus looked at his hands, then back at Joe. "Let's see . . . today being Thursday, I'm going to guess that you've just heard about the Fourth Law of Stratospheric Success?"

Joe nodded. "Authenticity. And now I'm supposed to figure out some way to apply it."

Gus pursed his lips thoughtfully. "Well. Seems to me, perhaps you just did."

Joe stared at Gus for what seemed like an entire minute.

Gus smiled back, unblinking.

"It's you, isn't it?" Joe said softly. "*You're* the Connector."

Gus unfolded his hands, leaned back in his chair, scratched his head, looked out the window, then looked back at Joe and spread out his hands. *Ya got me.*

"I met our friend Pindar thirty-five years ago. Introduced him to Sam Rosen a few years later.

"A few years after that, I invested a few dollars and bought both men hot dogs at a neighborhood stand I knew about.

94

That hot dog lunch turned out to be a very productive investment."

He gave Joe a moment to digest this information, then continued.

"A little over ten years ago, I introduced Ernesto Iafrate and his wife to Debra Davenport, the woman who sold my wife our house. Unless I miss my guess, you probably heard her speak earlier today."

Dazed, Joe just nodded.

"A few years later, when some young friends of mine wanted to form their own software company, I introduced them to Sam, who gave them financial advice. Sam, Pindar and I invested in Nicole Martin's little venture, and we did well, just as we did with Iafrate's Café."

Noting Joe's open-mouthed stare, Gus laughed a little self-consciously. "I don't know, I just keep finding good horses to back. I've always been pretty lucky that way."

He looked Joe in the eye, and Joe understood that he was saying he considered Joe to be one of those "good horses," too, and that it had nothing whatsoever to do with luck.

"I—I don't get it," Joe blurted out. "Forgive me for putting this so bluntly, but you must be worth millions!"

Gus gazed at Joe with an intensity Joe had never seen in the old man's face before. "This is something I consider very, very private, but I'd like to share it with you now, and trust that this will be confidential, between us. My net worth."

Joe nodded.

Gus named a figure.

Joe's knees went weak. "But why do you still work here?

Why do you still work at all?" Before Gus could answer, Joe held up one hand. "No, don't tell me. I'll bet I know."

He thought about Gus's long, rambling conversations, his easy manner with potential clients, his erratic, extended vacations. He smiled.

"You just love what you do. You love talking with people, asking them questions, learning all about them, finding ways you can help them, serve them, fill a need, share a resource . . ."

Gus stood up, ambled over to the coatrack, retrieved his tweed jacket and winked at Joe. "An old man's gotta have *some* fun."

As Gus walked to the elevator door, Joe smiled and called out, "See you at lunch."

Gus turned and looked back at Joe, puzzled. "Lunch?"

Joe chuckled. "Oh, no, this time I have it figured out. You're the Connector, right? So, you're my lunch date at Pindar's tomorrow! The Friday Guest!"

"Ahhh, the Friday Guest." Gus gave a little laugh. "Me? No, it's not me." He laughed again and stepped into the elevator, talking to himself as he went. "The Friday Guest. Now *that* should be fun."

12: The Law of Receptivity

Friday at twelve o'clock sharp, Joe rapped briskly on the front door of the great stone mansion. He glanced up at the gathering clouds and slipped his hands into his pockets for warmth. Today was the kind of late September day that held more hints of approaching winter than of departing summer.

He was about to knock a second time when the door swung open and Rachel appeared.

"Joe! Come on in," she said, leading him into the study. "The Old Man had an unexpected phone call. If you don't mind waiting here, he'll be down in just a few minutes."

Joe looked around the oak-paneled room with its muted tones and its smells of leather and old books.

"You're not going out today," Rachel said in answer to Joe's unspoken question. "Today's the day you dine here."

Joe noticed that Rachel said this as if it were part of an established sequence, something she'd explained many times before. "Today's the Friday Guest, huh?"

Rachel smiled. "Exactly."

"Can I ask you a question?" Joe had been itching to have

this conversation ever since Wednesday, when Pindar had told him Rachel's story.

"Sure."

"What's it like, working for Pindar?"

Rachel hesitated, then smiled at Joe. "Honestly?" She sat down in one of Pindar's wingback chairs. "It's been amazing."

In the year since she had first come to work at the stone mansion, Rachel had learned more about the art of good business than most entrepreneurs would pick up in a lifetime of experience. She learned about finance and philanthropy, negotiation and networking, resources and relationships—"Pindar's principles of cooperative commerce, from A to Z," she said with a grin.

And she applied all these lessons by throwing herself into the earnest study of her passion—the making of excellent coffee.

Starting with a long conversation at Ernesto's café, Rachel had explored the world of restaurant supply, carefully researching the most reliable supply lines to all the best equipment, such as commercial-scale roasters and grinders.

She also taught herself to source premium coffee beans from all over the world. She started by getting to know a few individual coffee farmers in Colombia whom she connected with through her Spanish teacher at college, who was Colombian. Quickly picking up the region's different Spanish dialects, she easily made additional contacts in the surrounding countries of Ecuador, Venezuela, Peru and Brazil. Soon she widened her network to other continents as well, establishing friendships with growers in Sumatra, Indonesia, Kenya, Yemen . . .

"Do you know how many coffee-producing countries there are on our little planet?" she asked.

Joe thought for a moment. "Twenty?"

"More than *three dozen*. And over the last twelve months, I've developed personal relationships with coffee growers in every single one of them."

Joe was stunned. With this extraordinary network, Rachel could bypass the brokers and middlemen and tap a worldwide supply of the highest quality coffee—at exceptionally low prices. And then there were all the people she'd served coffee to in Pindar's living room over the last twelve months, which brought her contacts with first-class expertise in every aspect of business from import/export to international financing to management and human resources.

In fact, if she wanted to, Rachel could probably walk out of this house and within forty-eight hours lay the groundwork for a global gourmet coffee empire!

"Oh, my gosh," Joe blurted out. "Of course!" He slapped himself on the forehead and laughed.

"Of course what?"

A big smile crept over Joe's face. He leaned back in his chair and pointed at Rachel. "Of course—*you*."

"Me," said Rachel.

"You. You've been here all week, so it never occurred to me. And it was right in front of my nose the whole time!"

Rachel arched her eyebrows. *Yes?*

Now Joe pointed at Rachel with the index fingers of both hands, like a pair of pistols. "You're the Friday Guest. Admit it!"

Rachel sighed and held up her hands, as if to say, *I give up, you win.* "Good guess!"

Joe beamed.

"But no dice."

Joe's smile faded.

Rachel cocked her head, listening. "Ah. His phone call's over." She got to her feet. "When you're ready, can you find your way to the terrace? He said you two will sit out and eat lunch while you wait for the Friday Guest to arrive."

She smiled at the look of consternation on Joe's face and quietly withdrew.

Joe slowly shook his head, then got up out of the comfortable chair and headed out to the terrace to join his mentor and await the Friday Guest . . . whoever that might turn out to be.

"So, what do you think about all this?"

For the past twenty minutes, the two of them had enjoyed the most wonderful lunch of cold cuts, fresh breads and an array of pickles, olives, relishes and the like. Joe counted five different types of mustard, and he had managed to sample every one of them. But he knew Pindar's question was not about the lunch spread. It was about everything he had seen and heard during the week.

Joe hesitated, then spoke carefully, as if stepping from stone to stone across a river. "I think . . . it all sounds, amazing.

Wonderful, really wonderful." He paused, feeling the spreading warmth of the late-September sun.

"And?" prompted Pindar.

"And I'm just not . . ." Joe took a big breath, and then let it out, unable to finish the thought.

"Let me see if I can help here," said Pindar. "When you were young, what did you learn about giving?"

Joe frowned in concentration.

Pindar interrupted his train of thought before it had even gotten started. "Don't think about it, Joe. Don't *try* to remember. Just tell me, when I say *giving*, what's the first thing that leaps to mind?"

"It is better to give than to receive—"

"Exactly! *It's better to give than to receive*, right? If you're a good person, that's what you do, you give. Good people give and don't think of receiving. But you, you think about receiving all the time, you can't help it. Which means you're probably not really a very good person . . . so why bother trying? All this giving stuff sounds great—for some people. For people like me, maybe, or Nicole, or Ernesto. But not for you. It's just not who you are."

There was a moment of silence.

"Is that how it is?"

Joe sighed. "Something like that," he admitted.

Pindar turned and looked out at the city stretching off to the west. He seemed pensive, almost sad. He continued looking into the distance as he resumed speaking.

"I want you to try something for me. I'm going to count to thirty, and while I count, I want you to slowly exhale. That's all; just exhale, and don't stop. Take a good breath in first, so you have plenty of air, okay? Now, breathe in . . . and . . . go!"

And as Pindar began counting, Joe began to slowly let his breath out. By the time Pindar had reached "nine," Joe was hunching forward and turning a bit pale. At "twelve" he straightened up and abruptly drew in a big gasping breath.

Pindar glanced at Joe.

"Couldn't get to thirty?"

Joe shook his head.

"What would you think if I told you it has been medically proven that it's healthier for you to exhale than to inhale? Would that make a difference?"

Puzzled, Joe shook his head again.

"No, of course not. You can't just go on exhaling forever, no matter what argument anyone gives you.

"What if I told you that it's better for your heart to relax than to contract? To just keep opening up, without squeezing down again. Would you give it a try?" This time he didn't even wait for an answer. "It's ridiculous, right? Of course it is. And so is that bit of traditional wisdom nonsense that you and I and everyone else had drummed into us.

"It's not *better* to give than to receive. It's *insane* to try to give and *not* receive.

"Trying not to receive is not only foolish, it's arrogant. When someone gives you a gift, what gives you the right to refuse it—to deny their right to give?

"Receiving is the *natural result* of giving. If you give and then try to stop the receiving that comes back, you're like King Canute watching the tide roll out and commanding it not to come back in. It *has* to come back in, just as your heart *has* to contract after relaxing.

"At this instant, all over the globe, all of humanity is breathing in oxygen and breathing out carbon dioxide. So is the rest of the animal kingdom. And right now, at this instant, all over the globe, the billions and billions of organisms of the plant kingdom are doing the exact opposite—they're breathing *in* carbon dioxide and breathing *out* oxygen. Their giving is our receiving, and our giving is their receiving.

"In fact, *every* giving can happen *only* because it is *also* a receiving."

And with that, Pindar abruptly stopped speaking and gazed again out at the city and mountains beyond.

Joe sat riveted to the spot, as if in the aftermath of an earthquake.

Every giving can happen only because it is also a receiving. . . .

For a full minute, neither spoke. Joe heard nothing but the confused rush of blood in his ears—it was as if he could hear the sounds of thoughts swirling in his brain. Then he became aware of his breathing—in, and out, in, and out, in, and out—and he laughed.

"A horse!"

Pindar turned and looked at him quizzically.

"A horse," Joe repeated. "To water. You can lead a horse to water . . ."

Pindar cocked his head and waited.

". . . but you can't force him to *take* the water you offer. That's the last law, isn't it? Receiving? *Choosing* to receive?"

Pindar said nothing, nor did he move. He just continued to watch and listen.

Joe's thoughts started coming in a rush.

"All the giving in the world won't bring success, won't create the results you want, unless you also make yourself willing and able to receive in like measure. Because if you don't let yourself receive, you're refusing the gifts of others—and you shut down the flow. Because human beings are born with appetite, nothing is more naturally geared toward being receptive than a baby, and if the secret of staying young, vibrant and vital throughout life is to hang on to those most precious characteristics we all have as children but which get drummed out of us—like having big dreams, being curious and believing in yourself—then one of those characteristics is being open to receiving, being *hungry* to receive, being *ravenous* to receive!"

And now Joe's eyes were shining, as were Pindar's, watching him.

"In fact, all those things I just mentioned—having big dreams and being curious and believing in ourselves—those are all *aspects* of being receptive, they're all the *same thing* as being receptive. Being open to receive is like . . ."

And here Joe seemed to grapple for a moment. He spread out his arms and looked upward, as if searching for a word big enough to convey his thoughts—

"It's like, *everything*!"

Joe stopped.

Pindar beamed at him for a moment, then spoke.

"The world certainly was designed with a sense of humor,

wasn't it? Inside every truth and every appearance, there's a bit of *opposite* tucked inside."

"Just to keep things interesting," Joe mused aloud.

"Yes," Pindar replied, nodding with delight, "that's an excellent way of putting it. Just to keep things interesting, things are always a bit the opposite of what they seem."

"So the secret to success," Joe went on, "to *gaining* it, to *having* it, is to give, give, give. The secret to *getting* is *giving*. And the secret to *giving* is making yourself open to *receiving*. What do you call this law?"

Pindar raised his eyebrows. "What would *you* call it?"

And Joe replied without hesitation: "The Law of Receptivity."

Pindar nodded thoughtfully. "Good."

They sat together in silence for a long moment, contemplating the Law of Receptivity and the glorious irony of creation that tucks its greatest truths carefully inside of paradoxes.

Joe had a sudden thought that nearly made him jump.

"My lunch hour's nearly over! Who were we supposed to see today?"

Pindar looked over at him. "Mmm?"

"Who were we supposed to see? You know, who was supposed to reveal the last law? The Friday Guest?"

Pindar smiled.

"Ah, the Friday Guest. That would be you, my friend." And he paused and said again, "That would be you."

The Fifth Law

THE LAW OF RECEPTIVITY

*The key to effective giving
is to stay open to receiving.*

13: Full Circle

That afternoon the mood was somber on the seventh floor of the Clason-Hill Trust Corporation. Third quarter was coming to an end, and all Joe's colleagues were doing the same thing he was. They were trying to conjure some last-minute miracles to bring in just a little more business.

Or in Joe's case, a *lot* more business.

But that business had not arrived. Carl Kellerman had called to confirm the bad news: Neil Hansen had indeed been awarded the fat contract Joe called the Big Kahuna, and Joe had not.

Joe sat at his desk gazing thoughtfully at his empty coffee cup while his coworkers began pulling on their coats and snapping their briefcases shut. It was already after five. Whatever else they might accomplish would have to wait for October and fourth-quarter business.

"You want to come in off that ledge and talk about it before you jump?"

Joe looked up to find Gus peering at him from his open

office door. Joe gave a half-hearted laugh and motioned for his friend to join him. Gus took a chair by Joe's desk, while Joe fiddled with a pencil.

"Well, Gus, I just lost the account of my career and blew my third-quarter numbers. I'm not even sure what'll happen to me now. And the really weird thing about it is . . ."

While Gus listened, he pulled his meerschaum from a vest pocket and poked at it.

"The weird thing is, of course I feel bad . . . but not as bad as I should. I mean . . . I never actually *tried* to get Pindar's help on this deal. I never even brought his name up to Carl Kellerman. I suppose I screwed up big time—but if I had to do it over, I think I'd do the same thing. You know?" He looked up at the clock on the wall. "Exactly one week ago, right at this moment, I was asking you for Pindar's phone number. And now . . ." He sighed. "Patience, I guess."

Gus pulled a small silver lighter from his pocket, put the meerschaum between his teeth, ignited the lighter with a soft *snick!* and held the flame to the pipe's hard white clay bowl. He puffed a few times until the pipe was well lit, then leaned back.

The man was actually smoking a pipe, right here in the office!

Gus winked at him. "Just a few puffs." He drew on the pipe, then held it away, peered into the bowl and poked at it with his forefinger. "You can't measure your success by whether or not you get the account. That's not the point."

"No? What is the point, then, Gus?"

Gus took another puff, blew three perfect smoke rings and

watched them fade away, then knocked the pipe's contents out into Joe's trash can.

"The point is not *what you do*. Not *what you accomplish*. It's *who you are*."

Suddenly Joe felt like crying. "I know. It's just . . ." He looked up into Gus's face and was struck by how much his kindly expression reminded him of Pindar's. "It's just, I hate to sound so pragmatic and mundane, but what good is all that if it doesn't generate any wins in the marketplace? I could be a saint and starve to death!"

Joe cast a forlorn glance around the office, looked up at the clock, and suddenly sat bolt upright.

"Ahhhh . . . the last law!"

Gus raised his eyebrows. "Mmm?"

"I'm supposed to apply the Law of Receptivity! The key to giving is being open to receive. But how am I supposed to do that? How do you go about being actively open to receive? 'Cause I'll tell you, Gus, I'm *already* open to receive, honestly— I mean, I am really, really open!" He sighed and hunched back in his chair. "At least I thought I was. But it looks like the only thing I'm receiving is the short end of the stick."

Gus leaned over and put his hand on Joe's shoulder. "Don't worry, Joe." He stood up. "Worrying about it does no one any good. You've had a long week. Go home to your wife. I'll stay and close up."

Something in Gus's manner made Joe's shoulders relax, and he felt his bleak mood dissipate slightly. He gave his older colleague a wan, tired smile. "Thanks, Gus. But you go ahead. I'll get it."

THE GO-GIVER

Gus shook his head and went to get his coat. "You're a different person than you were a week ago, Joe, you know that?" He walked to the elevator, pushed the DOWN button, and turned back just as the door slid open. "Although *this* Joe was already inside there, too. Just not quite visible yet." He smiled. "Good night, Joe."

"'Night, Gus. And . . . thanks."

Alone in the office now, his eyes closed, Joe sat, quiet. He could feel the daylight ebbing. Time to close up. He slowly got to his feet. He ambled over to the coffee urn, dumped out the shallow, bitter pool of late afternoon coffee, removed and discarded the cool, damp grounds, rinsed out the big metal cylinder, and began to wash the area around the percolator with wet paper towels.

As he washed the cups, drying and stacking them neatly in the cupboard, he thought of Rachel and her illustrious brew. He felt an odd smile of contentment bubble up from inside and spread over his face. He stopped moving and listened to the quiet stillness in the normally busy office.

What was it he was feeling? The quiet felt almost as if it were alive. Motionless, but listening. It felt . . . how would you describe it? *Receptive.*

The phone rang. Joe swiveled to stare at it, then at the wall clock. At six fifteen? On a Friday? He picked up.

"Hi, is this . . . Joe?" It was not a voice he recognized. "I can't believe you're still there."

"I'm sorry, have we . . . ?" Joe couldn't place the voice.

"No, you don't know me. Name's Hansen, Neil Hansen. Ed Barnes gave me your number."

"Who? Ed Barnes referred *me*? Are you sure you—?"

And then he remembered.

Ed Barnes. The competitor whose name he had given to Jim Galloway. The phone conversation Monday—his first day of homework. *Give more in value . . .*

"Wait," Joe stammered, "—the Neil Hansen that got that account with—?!"

"Listen," the man sounded frantic. "I'm in a real jam . . ."

Joe couldn't believe his ears. The guy who had nailed the BK account without breaking a sweat—an arch-competitor, referred by yet *another* competitor—was now on the phone with Joe because he was "in a jam"?!

". . . and Ed said it was a long shot, but I might as well give you a call, that you might know someone—that you'd given him a great referral. I've got a guy about to call me back who works with this huge account—I'm talking seriously huge—and he's in a major bind. This account's lost their supplier and they need someone fast, 'cause they have this major thing lined up."

"Who's the account?" Joe asked.

He heard the man pause on the other end. "You won't believe me when I tell you."

He told Joe the name of the account.

For a moment, Joe couldn't breathe. It was a name next to which the Big Kahuna would seem no more than a minnow.

This was not a Big Kahuna.

This was a *humongous* Kahuna.

Joe felt dizzy. "What do they need?" he asked faintly.

"Hang on a sec, it's them calling now . . ."

Neil Hansen clicked off the line for a moment and Joe paced as he waited. After ten or fifteen of the longest seconds Joe had ever experienced, the voice came back on the line.

"Okay, now *they're* hanging on a sec. All right, here's what we got. They're buying three international hotel chains and consolidating them all under one roof, rebranding them with a strong emphasis on business conferences and resorts—and kicking the whole brand off by relaunching a luxury cruise line they purchased as part of the whole package—get this, in *three weeks.*"

Joe was afraid to ask. "And?"

"And, okay—last minute, they lost a critical concession. The supply people they were working with started getting funny with their pricing structure and finally had to pull out. None of the other suppliers we've tried to put them together with can possibly meet their scale or their quality standards. None of the other guys are big enough, and frankly, none of them are good enough. Whoever can make this happen is gonna be sitting on an amazing package—but I can't find anyone who can pull it off, not on this scale, price and schedule."

"What's the concession?" Joe almost whispered.

The other man's voice came back with a defeated, tired, Friday-afternoon tone. "Premium, top-shelf coffee. I'm talking hundreds of *thousands* of customers. I'm talking high,

I mean, *mega-high* quality, at impossibly high volume. Three weeks! *Three weeks!!* Nobody's come close!"

Joe took a long, slow breath, then sat down slowly in his chair.

He smiled.

"You know," he said, "I just might know someone."

14: The Go-Giver

The young woman emerged from the parking garage, blinking in the bright August sunlight. "You'll do fine, Claire," she murmured to herself for the third time that morning. She'd been communicating with this company for a few weeks now, but it had been all by phone and email. Today she was going to meet the man himself.

"You'll do fine," she repeated and headed down the block.

Claire had done quite a bit of research on this young company in the past few weeks, hoping to gain some insight into exactly what might have catapulted it into such amazing overnight success. It was not quite a year since one of the company's founders had had the good fortune to land the huge contract that launched the business she was about to visit into its stratospheric rise. "One of those sweetheart deals that comes along once in a lifetime, if then," was how one magazine article had described it—yet in the ten months since, he and his two partners had come into one good stroke of luck after another.

As young as he was, there was already a reputation circulating about his having a "golden touch."

Claire arrived at the address she'd been given, a converted

factory building in the city's old garment district, surrounded by boutique grocery markets and loft apartments. She peered through the door and sure enough, there was the name, hand-carved into a large wooden sign in the quaint tile foyer:

RACHEL'S FAMOUS COFFEE
FIFTH FLOOR

She leaned back and glanced up, counting the floors. The fifth floor . . . that would be the top floor. The sun's glare made her a little dizzy.

"Doesn't look like their success has gone to their heads," she mused as she stepped through the tiny foyer and into the ancient elevator.

The receptionist at Rachel's Famous Coffee greeted Claire with a warm smile and directed her down a long hall to a door bearing the single word "Brainstorming." She knocked twice softly, then twice again with more assurance.

The door swung open as she heard a man's voice exclaim, "Come in!" A beaming, spectacled, round-faced man in his late thirties ushered her into the spacious conference room as he shook her hand.

"You must be Claire," said the man. "I'm Hansen. Neil Hansen. It's so good to meet you. My partners and I appreciate all the hard work you've put into your proposal."

Claire nearly gasped. The huge polished hardwood conference table in the center of the room was covered with an elaborate scale model of what looked like a tiny mountainside settlement. On the outskirts of the village, a bank of wind-powered turbines drove a nearly invisible irrigation system that snaked through a series of tiered fields. The designer in Claire marveled at the simplicity and efficiency of the whole thing. It was stunning.

"Thank you very much, Mr. Hansen." Claire glanced up at the wall on the other side of the table and saw that it was covered with breathtakingly beautiful photographs, all of them black and white shots of children of varying ages and modes of dress.

The man followed her gaze and smiled warmly. "Amazing, aren't they? There's no force more powerful than the trust in a child's face." He walked around the table with Claire as she took in photo after photo. "Many of them are the children of our partners in the different regions where we do business.

"Rachel took all these herself, on her last trip," he added. "She'd be here to meet you, too, but she's out of the country right now, back in Central America nailing down some key connections for a big project we're launching later in the fall—big project, I'm talking *seriously* huge. But hey, you're here to see my other partner anyway, yes?"

Claire nodded.

"Why don't you go ahead in," said Neil Hansen, gesturing to a connecting door to the next office. "He's expecting you."

"Claire, welcome! Thanks for taking the time to see me," said the third founding partner of Rachel's Famous Coffee.

"It's an honor, sir," Claire replied, as she wondered, "Why is *he* thanking *me*?"

"Please, call me Joe. If you say 'sir' I won't know who you're talking to!"

Claire smiled. Despite her nervousness, something about the man's voice had put her curiously at ease. "All right . . . Joe."

"Thank you," said Joe. He showed her to a chair, then took a seat himself. "Claire, I want you to know that we all genuinely appreciated your proposal. It's obvious you put a great deal into it."

He paused briefly.

"I need to let you know," he continued, "that we've decided to give the fall marketing campaign to your competition."

There it was, the moment Claire had been preparing for all morning, yet it still hit her like a thunderclap.

"I . . . well, I appreciate your telling me in person."

"You're not surprised?"

"How could I be, sir—I mean, Joe? They're a big firm and I'm a solo freelancer. The fact is, they have a lot more to offer you than I do."

"Actually," Joe replied, "with all due respect, we don't think so. More experienced, yes, and they're excellent at what they do. But frankly, Claire, you're very talented—and what's more, you've got heart."

"Heart?" Claire was confused.

"I just told you that we're giving this contract to your competition. Your response was to thank me and give them a compliment. You've got heart.

"In fact," Joe continued, "that's why I asked you to meet with us today. The campaign we're giving your competition is an important one. But we've got another project that, in the big scheme of things, is even more so.

"My partners and I have started a foundation that is about to launch a major international initiative. The purpose of the Rachel's Famous Coffee Foundation is to work with indigenous communities throughout Central America, Africa, Southeast Asia, all the coffee-producing countries in the world, helping to create community-based, self-sufficient business cooperatives."

He paused a moment to let Claire absorb what he was saying.

"This project is going to make a genuine, lasting difference for communities all around the world. It's going to take a significant amount of money to fund it properly. We need someone to design and coordinate the global effort to raise that money. I know this is a little different from what you've been doing up until now, but we'd like that someone to be you, if you're interested."

Claire was too thunderstruck to say a word.

Joe nodded as if Claire had spoken, and continued. "Of course, you'll need to think about this. What I'd really like is to have my wife, Susan, tell you more about it. She's the smartest civil engineer I know, and we've been lucky enough to persuade her to leave her position with the city and join us. *And*"— he glanced at his watch—"she'll be meeting me in a few minutes downstairs to go for lunch. Do you have time to join us?"

Claire paused, looking for the right words.

"Sir—Joe . . ."

Joe said nothing, but gave a gentle nod as if to say, *Go on*.

"How—how do you *do* all this?"

Joe looked slightly puzzled. "Do all what?"

"How do you create these amazing situations? It's not even a year since you and your partners started this whole thing. Most people would still be struggling just to get a new business off the ground, and you're already launching massive projects and having a worldwide impact.

"I guess what I'm saying is, I'm very flattered by your offer, and I'm certainly interested in learning more about your project—*very* interested. But what I'm most interested in is learning how you do what you do. It's got to be more than just being lucky or in the right place at the right time. Whatever it is you three have tapped into, I'd sure love to know what it is and how it works!"

For a moment, Joe seemed lost in thought. Claire was starting to wonder if she'd been too bold and perhaps offended him, when he took a deep breath and spoke.

"A question like that deserves a clear, complete answer. And I promise to give you exactly that—over lunch, if you're free to join us. Have you ever been to Iafrate's? It's our favorite."

Claire heard herself say, "Thank you," and, "No, I haven't . . ."

Joe smiled as he got to his feet. "There's someone there I'd like you to meet."

THE FIVE LAWS OF STRATOSPHERIC SUCCESS

THE LAW OF VALUE

*Your true worth is determined by
how much more you give in value than you take in payment.*

THE LAW OF COMPENSATION

*Your income is determined by
how many people you serve and how well you serve them.*

THE LAW OF INFLUENCE

*Your influence is determined by
how abundantly you place other people's interests first.*

THE LAW OF AUTHENTICITY

The most valuable gift you have to offer is yourself.

THE LAW OF RECEPTIVITY

The key to effective giving is to stay open to receiving.

ACKNOWLEDGMENTS

The conception, gestation and birth of a book is a miraculous process, and the word "acknowledgment" doesn't even begin to do justice to the creative and supporting roles played by so many. Our deepest appreciation goes out:

To our friends who read the manuscript at different stages and offered their insights, wisdom, enthusiasm and suggestions: Scott Allen, Shannon Anima, Brian Biro, George Blumel, Jim "Gymbeaux" Brown, Angela Loehr Chrysler, Leigh Coburn, John Milton Fogg, Randy Gage, Tessa Greenspan, John Harricharan, Philip E. Harriman, Tom Hopkins, James Justice, Gary Keller, Pamela McBride, Frank Maguire, Dr. Ivan Misner, Paul Zane Pilzer, Thomas Power, Nido Qubein, Michael Rubin, Rhonda Sher, Brian Tracy, Arnie Warren, Doug Wead, Chris Widener and Lisa M. Wilber.

To Ana Gabriel Mann, who scrutinized the manuscript at every stage and buoyed the project with her belief at every breath. Ana, you are the inspiration for the Law of Authenticity.

To Thom Scott, who exemplifies the Law of Influence and whose strategic genius and Internet wizardry have generously guided *The Go-Giver*'s path into the world.

To Bob Proctor, stratospheric mentor to multitudes and the original inspiration for "Pindar."

To our amazing team at Portfolio: Adrienne Schultz, Adrian Zackheim, Will Weisser and Courtney Young. May your continued success be determined by how many you serve and how well you serve them! This little book could not have found a better home.

To the most wonderful agents in the world, Margret McBride, Donna DeGutis, Anne Bomke and Faye Atchison—agents, editors, champions extraordinaire and exemplars of the Law of Value.

To our many colleagues and friends, unnamed and unnumbered but not unremembered, who've contributed to our lives and helped form the ideas at the heart of *The Go-Giver*.

And most important, to you, our faithful reader and Friday Guest. Go give—and remember to stay open to receiving.

A NOTE FOR THE 2015 EDITION

Since *The Go-Giver* first came out in 2007, there have been so many more people involved in helping it grow. We cannot possibly thank you all here, but we hope the following few will represent the many. Our gratitude goes out:

To all those on our always incredible Portfolio team who have joined the effort since we wrote our original acknowledgments, including: Jacquelynn Burke, Brooke Carey, Maureen Cole, Natalie Horbachevsky and Brittany Wienke.

To Gilles Dana for our audio versions; to all the agents and editors and translators and publishers too numerous to list who have championed our little story in nearly two dozen

editions around the world; and to Jack Covert, Lisa Earl Mc-
Leod and a gazillion others for helping get out the word right
here in the States.

To Kathy Tagenel, whose never-ending good cheer and inexhaustible talents keep Go-Givers International going and
so many other plates spinning at once.

To Harriet Dominique, Larry Kendall, Arlin Sorenson,
Randy Stelter and all our other *personal walking ambassadors:* you are not simply the best, you are *stratospherically* the
best.

A *Go-Giver*
Discussion Guide

Many of our readers have explored *The Go-Giver* together in their book clubs, business study groups, houses of worship and community groups, or among friends and family. The questions below may be helpful in guiding your discussions.

1. Joe first visits the Chairman because he is hoping to get "some big guns" to win back the deal he just lost, and he believes Pindar will give him "clout and leverage" (p. 3). Does he get what he went looking for? If so, how? And if not, why not?

2. Joe is surprised at how easily he gets in to see Pindar, and further surprised when Pindar remarks on how often successful people are willing to share their secrets with others (p. 8). Have you found this to be true? How would you go about meeting someone you'd want to learn from?

3. Pindar tells Joe, "The world treats you more or less the way you expect to be treated. . . . In fact, you'd be amazed at just how much *you* have to do with what happens *to* you" (pp. 13–14). Do you agree? Why? or why not? Can you think of examples of how this may be true?

4. Pindar gives Joe one condition for showing him the Five Laws: that he has to implement each one by applying it right away, the same day he learns it (p. 16). Does Joe fulfill that condition fully, for every one of the Five Laws? And if so, how?

5. Ernesto explains what makes a bad restaurant, a good restaurant, and a great restaurant (p. 26). What businesses do you know of that fit Ernesto's definition of greatness? How do they do it?

6. Ernesto tells Joe "Does it make money?" is a great question to ask; it's just a bad *first* question (p. 27). Why? What happens if you make that the first question?

7. Nicole says she used to believe that there are two types of people in the world: those who get rich, and those who do good (pp. 44–45). Do you see an inherent conflict or contradiction between being a good person and being a wealthy person, or to put it another way, between giving and receiving?

8. Nicole tells Joe that *"being broke and being rich are both decisions,"* that you make them up in your head and "everything else is just how it plays out" (p. 45). Do you agree? Why? or why not? Can you think of examples of how this may be true?

9. Why does Joe say he felt "like an idiot" when he served coffee to everyone on his floor (p. 51)? Gus comments, *"Sometimes you feel foolish, even look foolish, but you do the thing anyway."* Have there been times when you felt foolish but did the thing anyway, and seen that ultimately lead to great reward?

10. Pindar says the three universal reasons for working are: to *survive*, to *save*, and to *serve* (p. 55). Another way of describing this might be: to *have a job*, to *pursue a career*, or *to follow a calling*. Most people focus on the first, Pindar adds, but the genuinely successful focus on the third. Whom do you know who falls into that latter category? Where do you see yourself on that spectrum?

11. Sam seems to disparage the concept of win-win, even though that in itself is a wholly positive concept (p. 63). What is it exactly that Sam is cautioning Joe about here? Have you seen examples of that in your own life?

12. Sam tells Joe that what makes an influential person influential is not money, position or accomplishments, but how much they put others' interests ahead of their own (p. 64). Do you agree? Why? or why not? What well-known people can you think of who exemplify this? Whom do you know personally who does?

13. Why does Debra Davenport describe her husband's walking out on her, obviously a very painful and difficult experience, as a "gift" (p. 80)? What does she mean when she says it took her a full year "to unwrap, open, understand, and use" that gift—and that she now wants to share that gift with everyone in her audience (pp. 80–81)?

14. In chapter 13, Gus tells Joe he is "a different person than you were a week ago" (p. 112). Is this true, and if so, how? If you had to identify a single moment in the story when he makes this shift, what would it be?

15. At the end of the week Joe gets a phone call out of the blue that will turn out to change his life (p. 112). In our experience, things that seem to happen "out of the blue" are rarely as random as they seem. Can you identify the moment, earlier in the story, that planted the seed for that call to take place?

16. Three of Pindar's friends—Ernesto, Nicole and Sam—spell out the first three Laws to Joe, directly and explicitly. The Fourth Law comes a little more indirectly as part of Debra Davenport's public talk. And nobody tells Joe what the Fifth Law is, or even what it's called. Why do you think the authors had Pindar set things up this way?

17. When he meets Ernesto, Joe at first has no idea that he is one of Pindar's masters of stratospheric success. The same thing happens the following day with Nicole. Do you think the authors did this to make a deeper point? There are at least four other characters in the story whose full role eventually surprises Joe. Can you identify those four?

You'll probably come up with your own questions, too, and we would love to hear them! You can share your discussion questions at www.thegogiver.com/discussion.

Q&A with the Authors

Since the initial publication of *The Go-Giver*, we've received thousands of great questions from readers, via email and in person. Getting to hear readers' inquiries has been one of the best things about the experience of writing and sharing this book. Here are some of the most frequent questions we are asked, along with our best effort at answering them.

How did the two of you come to collaborate in writing this book?

Bob had been a top sales professional and speaker, John an educator and a successful entrepreneur. Both were published authors. We met when John edited some of Bob's writings and we discovered that although our backgrounds were quite different (Bob was formerly a Golden Gloves boxing champion; John was a concert cellist), our values and views on how the world works were completely in sync.

How did the story come together?

Bob had the idea of writing a parable titled *The Go-Giver* and brought it to John, along with a few dozen pages of notes and drafted scenes. The central idea—the power of being a giving person and adding value to others' lives—resonated strongly with both of us. We let the story unfold from there. Once we got rolling, John would sketch out a scene or chapter, email it to Bob and we would get on the phone and jam on it together. Sometimes we have a hard time remembering who came up with which line.

Where did the Five Laws come from?

The principles Pindar teaches Joe were drawn from our experiences and observations, in business and in life, and from the wisdom and experience of teachers too numerous to count. They didn't originate with any one particular teacher, school, religion or philosophy, and certainly are not original with us. They're an integral part of what it means to be a human being.

We didn't have these Five Laws worked out when we started writing, or even know there would be five. When we got to the end, we were as surprised and excited by how the Fifth Law emerged as Joe was. In fact, the scene where Joe works that out is awfully similar to what it was like the day we wrote that scene.

Is *The Go-Giver* purely fictional or is it based on a true story?

Most of the characters in the story are based (albeit loosely) on people we know. Many of the experiences in the story, while fictional, reflect experiences we've either witnessed or had ourselves. In a few cases, literally: Pindar's conversation with Larry King on page 9 is one Bob actually had with King, and the passage about the secret to Pindar's successful marriage on page 78 is a conversation Bob had with his dad at the age of twelve.

While Joe's story is fictional, what happens to him is not. We've seen it happen in real life hundreds of times, and we'll bet you have, too.

Are you saying that being a go-getter is a bad thing?

Not at all. We love go-getters; they take action and get things done! What we're saying is that being a go-getter *without* having your focus on giving value to others is bound to be an exercise in frustration, as Joe experiences at the beginning of the story.

Being a go-giver actually makes you a more effective go-getter. In fact, everyone we know who is a genuine go-giver is also a powerful go-getter.

If there is an opposite to a go-giver, it is not a go-getter but the person who is constantly on the lookout for how the world can serve them and who puts that focus in front of everything else—you might say, a go-*taker*.

Is the moral of this story that "nice guys/gals finish first"?

It's not about being nice. Being a nice, genuinely kind person is great in itself and it helps build strong relationships, but it won't necessarily make you successful. There are plenty of people who are nice yet who are also struggling financially.

What we're saying is that success is the result of specific habits of action: creating value, touching people's lives, putting others' interests first, being real, and having the humility to stay open to receiving.

I've always given to charities. Does that make me a go-giver?

This is a tricky one. People often hear "giving" and think of giving money and charitable contribution. Giving gifts of charity is a wonderful and righteous action in itself—but that's not what we mean by being a go-giver and we're not necessarily talking about giving *financially*. As Arianna Huffington puts it so beautifully in her foreword, by "giving" we mean "being a giving person, *period:* one who gives thought, gives attention, gives care, gives focus, gives time and energy—who gives *value* to others."

But isn't it a lot easier to be a giver after you've become rich and successful?

Actually, it's the other way around. Being a giving person is *how* you become rich and successful (however you define those two words) in the first place. You don't need money to be a giving person. The process starts simply by adding value to other people's lives, right now, in any way you can, and it builds from there.

Does being a go-giver mean you're not interested in making a profit?

Quite the contrary. Go-givers typically make a great profit because they provide an abundance of value and a fantastic experience to their customers and clients. The key is where you place your principal focus. If you are focused on profit first, you will probably miss all sorts of opportunities to provide great value. When your focus is on your customers' experience, healthy profits tend to result.

Here's how we put it in *Go-Givers Sell More* (our handbook of *The Go-Giver*'s principles for salespeople): "Money is an echo of value. It is the thunder to value's lightning." The value comes first; the money you receive is the natural result.

My business is still small and struggling. How do I implement the Law of Value without giving away the store?

You don't have to be a high-end business or deal in luxury goods to add stratospheric value. Ernesto's "great restaurant" example could be a fine dining establishment, but could just as easily be a sandwich counter or neighborhood coffee shop. A focus on providing exceptional value is behind the success of high-end Mercedes-Benz and low-fare Southwest Airlines. Value is *value*, not price. Ernesto won acclaim as the "best dining experience in the city"—with *hot dogs*.

Does being a go-giver mean I should consider giving away my products or services for free?

While giving something away for free to begin or build upon a customer relationship can be a great marketing strategy, that's not being a go-giver. Ernesto charged for his hot dogs; Nicole's software has a price tag. And you can be sure that when Pindar gives a keynote speech or coaches a Fortune 500 CEO, he charges a healthy fee.

Being a go-giver doesn't mean you shouldn't profit from your work. If it did, there would be a lot of cold and hungry go-givers!

I'm confused by the Law of Compensation. Is Nicole saying that being a good person doesn't really matter?

Being a good person (however you define that) matters a great deal. It's just not what determines your income. Money is not a measure of your goodness or worthiness; it is a measure of your *impact*.

Does placing another person's interests before your own mean being self-sacrificial?

A "giving spirit" is not one of self-sacrifice, codependence or martyrdom. Placing others' interests before your own, "making your win about the other person," as Sam says, doesn't mean negating your own needs and interests. It means trusting that when you focus on others, your needs will be taken care of, too. And as people come to know you as someone who has others' interests first, that's exactly what will happen!

I love the idea of living and working this way, but doesn't it take longer to get real results?

Success in any endeavor naturally takes time to bring to full fruition. That said, taking a go-giver approach often brings about positive outcomes in *less* time, not more. Reader after reader has told us that when they made a conscious shift from a *me* focus to an *other* focus in their lives, dramatic and sometimes immediate results followed.

When Ernesto says you just give and don't think about the results, isn't that naïve? I mean, how can you *not* think about the results?

We are all human, which means we're all driven by self-interest. And we're not saying you should change that even if you could (which you can't). What we're suggesting is that you simply set your self-interest to the side.

We do something like this every time we watch a film. We know it's only a movie, but in order to enjoy the story we *willingly suspend our disbelief.* We still know that what's up on the screen isn't really happening, but by setting that knowledge temporarily to the side, we allow ourselves to feel the full emotional impact of the experience.

As a go-giver you do something quite similar, only in this case you *willingly suspend your self-interest.* You don't deny it, suppress it or try to eliminate it; you just defer it for the moment—which allows you to focus fully on the other person.

The picture you paint of the path to success seems awfully simple; isn't there a good deal more to it in real life?

Yes and no. Yes, things are greatly simplified here in order to tell the story. (This is a parable, after all, not a novel.) Still, the success won by the characters in these pages is not necessarily as simple as it might seem. The catalyst that brought Debra Davenport's career to life was her authenticity, but that came only after decades of life experience and a solid year of focused, difficult, full-time effort. Same with Ernesto: yes, he gave people an unforgettable dining experience, but that also included developing excellent kitchen and leadership skills.

Are you saying that all you need to do is give and give and eventually you'll receive, like magic?

Being a go-giver doesn't preclude dedicated effort and a sound business plan, and it doesn't mean simply doing random good deeds and expecting to be rewarded for them. (Helping an elderly woman cross the street is a great thing to do, but it's not a business strategy.)

The Quakers have a wonderful saying: "When you pray, move your feet." Both Ernesto and Nicole started out with very practical business models that they worked hard at: selling hot dogs, designing and marketing software. So did Sam (developing an insurance clientele), Debra (selling houses), and Claire (marketing her graphic design and advertising services). The Five Laws aren't magic; genuine success still takes work, but it becomes work you love.

Am I the only one who has a tough time with the Law of Receptivity?

You are definitely not alone! A lot of readers have told us that they felt an easy affinity with the first four laws but found *staying open to receiving* challenging and uncomfortable. "I'm still working on that last law" is something we've heard again and again.

Yet it's so crucial. The Five Laws are like four fingers and thumb. Trying to implement the first four principles without practicing the fifth is like trying to use a tool with just your fingers and no thumb. (Try it sometime with a hammer, pen or needle and thread.)

Many of us have learned to view giving and receiving, altruism and self-interest, as two conflicting and inherently contradictory states. But one can't operate effectively without the other—just like inhaling and exhaling. As Joe says, if you don't let yourself receive, you shut down the flow.

A great way to practice the Law of Receptivity: the next time someone pays you a compliment, instead of getting all embarrassed and denying it or saying "Oh, it's nothing," just *receive* it! Smile, say thank you and notice how you feel as you receive.

Doesn't it say in the Bible that it's better to give than to receive?

While Bob's background is Jewish and John's is Christian, we both share a deep respect for all faith traditions. As we get this question so often, we thought it might be helpful to have John address this one specifically.

Actually, the Bible doesn't say that. What it says (in Acts of the Apostles) is that "it is more *blessed* to give than to receive." The Greek word *makarios* (blessed), which is the same word used in the Eight Beatitudes (blessed are the meek, blessed are the merciful, blessed are the peacemakers, et cetera), carries these meanings: *fortunate, rewarded, prosperous, rich, happy.* In other words, when you focus on giving you end up more abundantly rewarded than if you had focused on receiving.

At its root, *makarios* means "grow larger" (like *macro*). When you give, you become a bigger person, in every way—more successful, more influential, more fulfilled.

Can you give us some examples of how people use the Laws in real life?

Pindar tells Joe he needs to implement each Law right away, the same day he learns it. We encourage our readers to do the same thing!

Applying the Laws needn't always be a big deal; it's something you can do in little ways, too, in the course of everyday life. When you set aside your own concerns for a moment and make a concerted effort to hear a team member's or customer's needs, goals and values, you're applying the Law of Influence. Tell a friend you're sorry for a mistake you've made, without excuses or defensiveness, and you're sharing the greatest gift you have to offer through the Law of Authenticity.

One reader, Christi Hegstad, told us that after reading the book she made a habit of doing one go-giver activity first thing each morning. "Send a card to someone just to let her know you're thinking of her. Leave a voice mail for a colleague wishing him a great day. Mail a newspaper clipping to a local businessperson recently highlighted. Write an unexpected testimonial. There are so many meaningful ways to become a go-giver, and it's a great opportunity for each of us to change the world for the better."

Do you think kids would understand the book? Is anyone teaching it in schools?

Yes—and yes! We often hear from parents who have given *The Go-Giver* to their children to read. One of the best analyses of the book we've ever read was sent to us by twelve-year-old Alex Hines, who concluded his report this way: "Pindar's exact age was impossible to guess and nobody knew his last name. Do you want to know why? Because the authors purposefully wanted you to see that it was a passed-down philosophy for success that everyone can learn and teach.

Now I can go by Pindar's laws and become a Pindar myself."
(You go, Alex!)

We've also heard from quite a few educators who are using the book in their classes, at every level from high school to grad school. One teacher, Randy Stelter, has been giving a course on *The Go-Giver* to the entire graduating class at Wheeler High School in Valparaiso, Indiana, every year since it came out. In fact, we have just released a *Go-Giver Curriculum Guide* based on Randy's work. You can find more information at thegogiver .com/curriculum.

I've finished reading *The Go-Giver*—is there more to the story? What else can I read about the go-giver way?

Go-Givers Sell More is a companion volume of sorts, a user's guide to *The Go-Giver* sprinkled with real-life experiences of people we know to illustrate the Five Laws. While nominally about sales, it's also about life and living.

The Go-Giver Leader (formerly titled *It's Not About You*) is another story that takes place in Pindar's town, where you'll meet Claire again and learn a bit about Pindar's early years. This book shows you the Five Keys to Legendary Leadership and what it means to be a go-giver in the context of working with others, not only for those in traditional "leadership" positions but for anyone—colleague, partner, parent or friend.

And more beyond those? It's possible. Giving is a big topic, and we suspect Pindar still has a lot to say.

And if you have other questions for us that we haven't answered here, by all means share them with us! You can reach us at www.thegogiver.com/contact.

BOB BURG is coauthor of the *Wall Street Journal* best-seller *The Go-Giver* and its companion volumes *Go-Givers Sell More* and *The Go-Giver Leader*. A former television personality and top-producing salesperson, Bob speaks to corporations, organizations and at sales and leadership conferences worldwide on topics at the core of *The Go-Giver* books. Addressing audiences ranging from sixty to sixteen thousand, Bob has shared the platform with some of today's top business leaders, broadcast personalities, coaches, athletes and political leaders, including a former U.S. president. He is also the author of *Adversaries into Allies* and the classic *Endless Referrals*, which has sold more than a quarter of a million copies and is still used today as a training manual in many corporations. He was named by the American Management Association as one of the Top 30 Most Influential Thought Leaders in Business for 2014.

JOHN DAVID MANN has been writing about business, leadership and the laws of success for more than thirty years. As a high school student, he led a group of friends in creating their own successful high school. After establishing himself as a concert cellist and prizewinning composer, he built a multimillion-dollar sales organization of more than a hundred thousand people before turning to writing and publishing. In addition to coauthoring *The Go-Giver* books with Bob Burg, John is also coauthor of the *New York Times* bestsellers *Flash Foresight* (with Daniel Burrus) and *The Red Circle* (with Brandon Webb) and the national bestseller *Among Heroes* (with Brandon Webb). His *Take the Lead* (with Betsy Myers) was named by Tom Peters and the *Washington Post* as Best Leadership Book of 2011.

Enjoy the entire Go-Giver series!

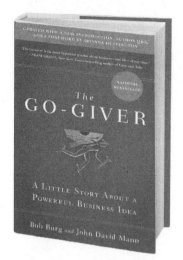

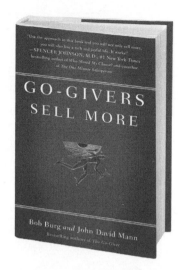

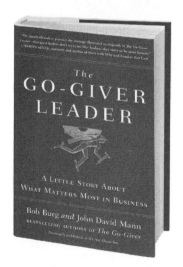

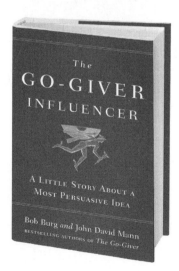

For more information, visit thegogiver.com.